MASTERSHIP

THE JOURNEY FROM BANKRUPTCY TO A NEW LIFE

MASTER LORNE DAVIDSON

◆ FriesenPress

Suite 300 - 990 Fort St
Victoria, BC, V8V 3K2
Canada

www.friesenpress.com

Copyright © 2017 by Master Lorne Davidson
First Edition — 2017

Attention – quantity discounts are available to your company, educational institution or writing organization for re-selling, educational purposes, subscriptions incentives, gifts or fundraising campaigns

Contact Information:
Website – www.mastershipjourney.com
E-mail – mastershipjourney@gmail.com
Linkedin – Master Lorne Davidson
Facebook.com – mastershipjourney
Phone – 604-542-3079

All rights reserved.

No part of this publication may be reproduced in any form, or by any means, electronic or mechanical, including photocopying, recording, or any information browsing, storage, or retrieval system, without permission in writing from FriesenPress.

ISBN
978-1-5255-1324-4 (Hardcover)
978-1-5255-1325-1 (Paperback)
978-1-5255-1326-8 (eBook)

1. BIOGRAPHY & AUTOBIOGRAPHY, PERSONAL MEMOIRS

Distributed to the trade by The Ingram Book Company

TABLE OF CONTENTS

FOREWORD
VII

INTRODUCTION
XI

CHAPTER 1
TAKING THE FIRST STEP
1

CHAPTER 2
CLASSES, LEARNING, AND TESTING
11

CHAPTER 3
BECOMING AN INSTRUCTOR AND CLUB OWNER
25

CHAPTER 4
A STARTING POINT
41

CHAPTER 5
A LEAP OF FAITH
53

CHAPTER 6
GOING COMMERCIAL—THE BIRTH OF THE BUSINESS
63

CHAPTER 7
GROWTH AND STABILITY
69

CHAPTER 8
WORLD CHAMPION
79

CHAPTER 9
SCHOOL NUMBER TWO—GROWTH, SEPARATION AND
THE PAIN OF EXPANSION
87

CHAPTER 10
CHALLENGES
97

CHAPTER 11
REUNITED
111

CHAPTER 12
ONWARD AND UPWARD
119

CHAPTER 13
HEALTH CHALLENGES
133

CHAPTER 14
DEVELOPING A PASSION FOR LEADERSHIP
141

CHAPTER 15
MASTERSHIP
151

ACKNOWLEDGEMENTS
165

PERSONAL LIBRARY
167

ADDITIONAL INFORMATION
173

This book is dedicated to my family, without whom none of what you're about to read would have been possible

—*Lorne Davidson*

FOREWORD

In the late summer of 2009, my son, Lawrence, informed me he didn't want to play hockey that fall. Having been a fan and player for my whole life, this was a bit of a shock to me. What?! A Canadian boy not wanting to play hockey?! What, pray tell, could you want to do instead? (His mother and I were not going to let him just veg out in front of a computer screen.) He told me he wanted to learn martial arts. Martial arts? That's just a fancy name for fighting, right? Now, I had nothing against fighting. (I played hockey, remember?) But I was taught how to fight by my dad, who grew up in a small town in Northern Ontario. It was more Don Cherry-like: Rock'em! Sock'em! What was there to learn? Well, having studied Aristotle and Aquinas, I was philosophical about it. It was his life, and if he wanted to ruin it by not learning the sweet science of hockey, he had to live with the consequences.

Now if you know anything about hockey parents, you know they will drive all over kingdom come to get their kids to an ice rink. But for martial arts? I don't think so. Not me anyway. However, not wanting to let on too much that I was less than enthusiastic about his choice of recreation, I suggested a karate school that I knew was somewhere near our local supermarket. Lawrence went online and googled "martial arts White Rock." He found the address of the karate school and another one that taught something called taekwondo. Hmm... OK, let's go. But let's go to the karate place, first; that seems more legit. (After all, I don't recall any movie called "Taekwondo Kid." Do you?)

Well, after circling the supermarket a few times trying to find the karate school, we gave up and started looking for the second school on our list: Seung-ri Black Belt Academy. We found it tucked behind a pet store or something. Without an appointment, we walked in and waited to chat with the white-clad young man instructing his white-clad charges. Being a singer and actor, I was struck by what appeared to be choreographed moves. (I would later learn these are called *forms*.) Also, the combination of aggressiveness and respect during the sparring. This is fighting? The only fighting I ever knew was the kind where you wanted to beat the crap out of someone because he pushed you too far on the playground or hit you too hard on the ice. Aggressive? Yes. Respect? Phtt...

But seriously, in that first brief encounter with taekwondo, I noticed something different and good. So did my son, apparently, for after our short meeting with the instructor, Lawrence informed me he didn't want to go see the karate school or any other martial arts school; he wanted to enroll here. It seemed like a hasty decision to me, but he was adamant; this was the school for him. Why? "Because they not only want you to learn how to do the moves and fight, but also be a good person." Well... I had no comeback. (Kids!) Surprised by the impression the school and the instructor made on Lawrence, Catherine and I were also impressed enough to enroll him at Seung-ri Black Belt Academy.

Fast forward to 2017. We have seven children who've attended Seung-ri, four of them achieving the rank of black belt, two of them becoming second degrees. The three older ones have moved on to college and work in California, but the four youngest continue to train there. Obviously, we are still impressed but no longer surprised. For since that initial trip I took with my son, we've gotten to know the heart and soul behind Seung-ri Black Belt Academy: the Davidson's, and in particular Lorne Davidson.

Over the eight years of our association with Seung-ri, I have had the boon of getting to know Lorne very well—some during academy events and tournaments, some on early morning walks along White Rock beach, but mostly through our regular Friday morning chats in my studio. During our discussions about faith, family, business, community, fitness, and music, bits of his story would come out. As his journey unfolded piecemeal to me, I was moved to a tremendous admiration and respect for this man who I now call a dear friend. If I might wax eloquent, Lorne truly is a phoenix who has risen out of the personal and financial ashes of an ill-concluded music career. But his fiscal recovery and the business success of Seung-ri are really only a part it. Starting over when nearly fifty in a field completely foreign to him—which demanded his total physical, mental, spiritual, and financial commitment—and armed with little more than his desire to succeed is truly remarkable, perhaps unbelievable. But he did succeed, and his story gives the rest of us hope that, in spite of age, obstacles, and even ourselves, we too can change and achieve in ways that seem unbelievable.

I'm not going to give you any advice except that you should turn the page and read Lorne's story. It was my privilege to read it first.

May God bless you always, Sir!

(By the way, that young instructor who made such a great first impression on my son was Robert Davidson, Lorne's son.)

Mark Donnelly

INTRODUCTION

"If somebody is gracious enough to give me a second chance, I won't need a third."

—Pete Rose

Do you believe in second chances, or maybe third or even a fourth? Do you believe you're worth one of those opportunities? If you received another chance to improve or make something different out of your life, what would you do with it? Every day is new and can be better than the day before. It can be as different from yesterday as we choose to make it. I firmly believe we are given that opportunity on a daily basis, but it's up to us to recognize it and exercise the option. From a personal perspective, I feel fortunate to have had that chance. I didn't recognize it at the time, but looking back over the past twenty years, it's clear. They say hindsight is 20/20, and in my case, that is completely accurate.

My second chance began in late February of 1996. It was a cold day, the sky was overcast, and a drizzling rain was falling—a typical February day on the West Coast of Canada. The weather set the mood for what my wife, Carole, and I were about to do. We were declaring personal bankruptcy. Walking into the bankruptcy offices, I don't think my head could have hung any lower. I felt more defeated than at any moment in my life. I was forty-eight years old and staring at my greatest failure. Even worse, it was through my own stubbornness, arrogance, and pride that I had dragged my wife and our three children into this moment with me.

How could this have happened? How could I not have seen it coming? Was I really that unaware? What had gone so wrong? Looking back now, I can sum it up in one word, "attitude," and describe it in one phrase, "rights versus privilege." For many years I carried the attitude that I had the right to do whatever I wanted; I was a child of the sixties and felt it was my right to be successful simply because I wanted to.

Over the years that have followed that February day, I have come to learn that, yes, on one hand I did have a right to do what I wanted to do—to learn and strive for success—but on the other hand, success was not a right in itself or ever guaranteed. Success is something that is earned by diligent, dedicated work; intelligent choices; and continual learning. If we are fortunate enough to achieve a certain degree of success, we should recognize it for the privilege that it is and treat it accordingly.

Flash ahead twenty years to October 21, 2016. The alarm in my hotel room was going off. It was 5:15 AM—time to get up and get ready for the day. I had been preparing for this, little by little, day by day, year by year, belt by belt, through successes, obstacles, and disappointments for over twenty years and I had been training daily for the past fourteen months—IT'S TESTING DAY. I was to test a second time for my sixth degree black belt at the ESPN Wide World of Sports complex in Orlando, Florida. I had often dreamt about this day over the last few years of my journey. To reach this moment, I had travelled to Korea to do a mid-term test there, and I had made countless trips to different US cities to complete my required mid-terms. All the while, I had competed in numerous tournaments around the country to keep myself in a state of preparedness. In June of 2016, I tested for my sixth the first time in Little Rock, Arkansas, and received a "no change." Here I was, once again preparing to reach for that goal.

Taekwondo literally translated means "the way *[do]* of the hand *[kwon]* and foot *[tae]*." It is Korea's national martial art and was designated as such on April 11, 1955. At the end of the Korean War, the first President of South Korea, Sung Man Yi, gave General Hong Hi Choi the idea of unifying the Korean people through the art of taekwondo after watching a demonstration of General Choi's 29th army division. The art of taekwondo focuses on strengthening the mental, physical, and spiritual aspects of the student and over my years of training I needed to develop in all three areas and continue doing so to this day.

The last five years had been some of the most challenging in my training. As a fifth degree black belt, I could only test at national or international events where there were two or more high rank judges in attendance—they needed to be seventh degree or above. Our national events were in Las Vegas in the spring, Little Rock in the summer for our World Championships and Expo, and Orlando in the fall, or internationally in Korea. Although I had remained on track throughout those five years, I had had more "no changes" (three mid-terms and one rank testing) than at any time along my journey. From 1996 to 2011, I had "no changed" two times, though I had never "no changed" when testing for rank previously. It seemed these last five years were a true test of my commitment and perseverance.

That October morning, I had no idea that all the disappointment and challenge would be rewarded. That day I would have the opportunity and honor of testing in front of the highest ranks in our organization. There were two Grand Masters and many members of our Founders Council, all eighth and ninth degree black belts. If I was fortunate enough to pass (I would not know until a few weeks later), I knew I would have been judged by the best. If I passed, I would become a Master Candidate. Then, upon receiving an invitation from the headquarters, I would be elevated to the status of Master Nominee. Once I had received that designation, I would be required to study and train for the next year, at the end of which I would be inducted as a Master Instructor in Songahm Taekwondo.

The amazing part of all this for me was that back in the spring of 1997, I had described this possibility to my instructor while sitting in a coffee shop in New Westminster, British Columbia, a little over a year after having declared bankruptcy. Here I was, ready to put the past twenty years of training on the line again. I was sixty-nine years old.

Over these twenty years of my second life, I have internalized three phrases. They have helped and guided me over that time. They have become my foundation, upon which I have come to understand how to work through the many challenges I faced after declaring bankruptcy. They have also helped give clarity to my actions during my previous life of forty-eight years, and act as a reminder for how I want to move forward. They are:

1. Rights versus Privilege

2. Quality of Life

3. We, the Fortunate Few

One of the phrases, *quality of life*, is something I've come to live by over the years. It speaks clearly to what my years of training and dedication to taekwondo have helped me learn. It also helped me understand another phrase, "We get out what we put in." For me, this definitely pertains to my quality of life. Most of us say that we would like to be healthier and more successful, and for forty-eight years I said the same thing. The author John Maxwell summed it up very well for me: "Everything worthwhile is uphill and everyone has uphill hopes and dreams, but most of us have downhill habits." That quote encapsulated the many years I spent in the music business. I'd had uphill hopes and dreams, but my habits sent me downhill. I had dreamed of success, but I hadn't taken the time to lay a proper foundation for it through my habits. At the root, I was a pretender. If I've learned anything over these past twenty years, it's that to achieve a better quality of life, I must be prepared to look critically at my actions.

> **"Rights vs. Privilege," "Quality of Life," and "We, the Fortunate Few"**

I grew to understand that, if I wanted a better life, I needed to continually work on improving the consistency of my actions and my personal habits, especially in discipline, perseverance, and self-control. To create uphill habits, we must support them with uphill effort. My three key phrases have become the foundational cornerstone that helped me rebuild my life. I came to realize that my uphill dreams of success have to be supported with consistent action.

Travelling and playing on the road for twenty years does not lend itself to positive, consistent action. The focus of my actions over those times was always on working with our management team to get the next gig while doing the best job possible on stage with the one at hand. There was seldom the time to step back and assess the work being done or plan what would be the best step to take next. It was simply: you're playing here this week and there next week and somewhere else the week after that, and don't mess up or get fired.

One of the key things I've come to learn throughout my training and studies in taekwondo is creating recovery time. It is imperative to give our bodies and minds time to recover after a hard workout or intense mental training; for that matter, even while we're training, there must be time to recover. During the years on the road, there was never a concept of recovery or assessment time—play, travel, rehearse, repeat—and that in the end would prove costly.

> **"Uphill dreams of success have to be supported with consistent action"**

I loved playing music and most of all loved singing harmony; that joy is something I remember fondly to this day. Playing music for me was a very special way of communicating. It was a very esoteric experience and looking back that was probably my error. I enjoyed everything about the life—playing and singing, performing, the travel, dead heading (driving without stopping, except for gas) from one town to another through the night just to get to the next gig, another new town with another experience waiting. Passing through the small towns along the way in the middle of the night, everything so peaceful and quiet. We were just a passing shadow, here then gone. The people we met and played for along the way—it was the way I wanted to live.

Somewhere along the line though I lost all the enjoyment that had so inspired me to start playing a bass guitar and learning to sing harmony; one day it just wasn't there anymore. I can't tell you when the travel, the thrill of getting new gigs, performing nightly, and climbing that ladder of success lost its luster, but it did. At the end it seemed the harder we worked, the more we lost ground and by the end I was just a shell of the man who had started with a dream and a love of playing music many years ago.

Over these past twenty years though, I have learned that lesson and made it a point to focus on recovery, improving my knowledge of nutrition, and my physical and emotional health. If I was to be a truly dedicated learner, then everything would be on the table at all times. With that in mind, I went back to school in the summer of 2016. I had not been in a daily classroom setting for over fifty years; yet at the age of sixty-nine, I became a North American Sports Medicine Certified Personal Trainer.

There are things we think we know, things we want to know, and things we need to know. In going back to school, I was able to improve my understanding of all those areas and about how to teach our staff and students to get the best out of their training. Becoming a certified personal trainer was something I had wanted to do for a few years but had struggled to find the time for. I thought it important to continually add to my knowledge of the human body. It was satisfying to be able to write and pass my test after so many years away from the classroom. My purpose in doing this was not only to improve the quality of my life but to be able share this knowledge with all our present students and our students yet to come.

Since 1996, my life has been filled with miracles and successes that I could never have imagined. I would never have believed someone if they had told me on that February day in 1996 that, if I could just be patient, work consistently on improving myself, find a way to work through the difficulties, study hard, and strengthen my faith, I would find success. I would have scoffed if they had said that by the time I was in my late sixties I would own two commercial martial arts school with over two hundred and fifty active students, and be debt-free other than the mortgages on a couple of condos and my car payment.

Today though, that is my life. And you know what? I feel like I'm just getting the hang of it. It's as they say: "It's not how we start; it's how we finish." It took me until I was well into my fifties to truly understand just how that phrase might apply to me. I've coined my third phrase in response: "We, the fortunate few." I've come to understand that we live in a part of the world where we have the opportunity every day to improve and make better choices. We have the opportunity to make those choices count. Every day, we have the chance to correct and improve on the mistakes we made the day before, and we are only restricted by the limitations we place upon ourselves.

This book is about what happened between February of 1996 and November of 2016. Although it's the story of my journey from being a bankrupt musician at forty-eight to a multi-school owner and Master Instructor in Songahm Taekwondo today, for me this book is also about so much more.

> **"It's not how we start; it's how we finish"**

This book is for all of us who want to believe that there are second chances, no matter our age or circumstance. Here is the tangible proof it can been done. I have been very fortunate, but I'm not special. I'm living proof that the opportunities are out there, available and waiting. Second chances are not just for other people. Remember, we are the fortunate few.

My sincerest hope is from this book you'll find some inspiration to help you begin to write your own story. I cannot tell you how many books, stories, and movies I've read and seen over these years, searching for the inspiration to carry me forward when times seemed dark. I continue to look for those stories that will move, motivate, and inspire me to remain open to the possibilities available in the human spirit. They help me re-evaluate how I can improve myself to make better choices, and they give me something to aspire to and believe in.

In the back of this book, I have included some of the most inspiring books and movies for your consideration; they definitely helped me. I hope you will find something that will help you, no matter your age or financial, emotional, or spiritual situation. My goal is to give you the drive, desire, and courage to act and bring your dreams into reality. Start today, right now. Evaluate where you are now. What are the positive things you have done? These are the things you can build on. Find out what are you passionate about and what interests you, and learn to explore what options are out there.

In what areas of your life could you use more self-discipline and focus? Do you believe in yourself, in your abilities and capabilities? Are you willing and prepared to learn, work, and do the research into how to improve your health or become more financially knowledgeable and secure? Whatever area you feel you need to improve in your life, let me encourage you: You can do it. Do whatever you need to do, and don't let your age or any adversity deter you. Don't let anything stand in your way. Trust me when I say that we all have the ability to overcome what we face. Not only are we capable of overcoming it, but we can thrive as we do it. If God led you to it, he'll lead you through it.

Are you willing to take the chance on yourself and commit to doing whatever it takes to effect the change you want to see? If you are still reading this, I believe you are, and I believe in the strength of the human spirit that is in you. As hard as it was at times, I learned to believe in myself too and, on that October day in 2016, I did pass my test. On June 21, 2017, I was inducted as a Master Instructor in Little Rock, Arkansas.

CHAPTER 1
TAKING THE FIRST STEP

"The journey of a thousand miles begins with the first step."
—*Lao Tzu*

In late summer of 1996, I gave in to pressure and did something that for the previous year I had been wholeheartedly resisting with everything I had: I attended a taekwondo class with my friend Bruce. He had been trying for ages to get me to go. Over that time, he had the support and encouragement of my wife, Carole. As strongly as he persisted, I resisted. I would find any excuse not to go. I was too tired. The class times were too late. It was too far to drive. I was too old… I had been a musician for over twenty years and I was a failure. What good would it do me to go to a taekwondo class?

During my years as a musician, I'd been witness to enough stupid, mindless bar fights to last a lifetime, so the last thing I was interested in was learning how to fight. Truth be told, at that time I was so angry and frustrated, dealing with my feelings of failure and worthlessness related to our recent bankruptcy, that going to a class to learn how to kick and punch felt like adding fuel to an already raging fire. I simply was not interested in stepping into that arena.

My decision to attend the class would dramatically change my life for the better. It is undoubtedly one of the best decisions I have ever made, even though I had to be dragged to it, kicking and screaming. As I was to find out later, Carole was the reason my friend was so persistent. Even before the bankruptcy, she had been asking Bruce if he could somehow get me involved. Her hope was that it might be a benefit and a stress release for me. She is a very wise woman, and I love her dearly. So, in that fateful moment in late August of 1996, I let go of my reticence and decided to attend one class. It was to be the beginning of a new chapter in my life.

Flashback to 1982, Carole and I were about to embark on what I hoped would be the beginning of, not only a new and better life, but also a new and successful career. I would be performing and playing music professionally with the love of my life. I had been playing the bar circuit throughout BC and Alberta for the past seven years. For most of those years, I played bass guitar and sang harmony. I was continually frustrated by what I perceived to be a lack of drive, focus, and professionalism in many of the players I performed with. Most were more talented than me, but it seemed they were more interested in drinking and partying than working to carve out a serious career in music. So after a couple years of watching me come home off the road frustrated and discouraged, Carole and I decided to combine forces and form a duo to start performing together. Carole had a beautiful voice, loved to sing, and was a good songwriter. I loved playing either bass or guitar and singing harmony. I felt that, with a little time on the road and some seasoning, we might have a chance at making a solid career in the music business. I was pursuing this dream when Carole and I first met in the spring of 1980 in Calgary. At that time, I was performing with a friend of hers, Brian, who lived in the apartment across the hall from her. Over that year, we fell in love and decided, against the wishes of her family, to get married. We eloped and tied the knot on October 11, 1980 (Canadian Thanksgiving), in Pincher Creek, Alberta with my friend and playing partner, Brian was best man.

For the first two years of our marriage, I worked on my craft, travelling and playing on the road while Carole kept the home fire burning by working in a local bank. On October 28, 1981, our first child, Tera Kathleen (Kat), was born. Life was good, for the most part. However,

MASTERSHIP

I was frustrated trying to find partners who had the same drive and ambition that I did. Brian, over this time, decided to move back to Ontario and I found another partner named Art. He had a great song list and played the guitar well. He also had a voice I was able to harmonize well with—but he had no great aspirations. As my frustrations continued to grow, Carole and I talked about what we saw as the risks and rewards of combining forces. In the end, we decided to give it a shot and see where it would take us. Carole quit her job at the bank and along with our daughter, Kat, we hit the road. For the first couple of years, we performed as a duo throughout small-town Alberta and Saskatchewan, working on our chops, with the odd gig at home in Calgary. During that time, we had our second child on March 16, 1984—another daughter, who we named Robyn Christine. Shortly after Robyn was born, Carole and I made a decision (which I pushed for) that, if we were to have any chance of truly establishing a career in music, we had to move to my hometown of Vancouver, BC.

In Vancouver, we would have greater opportunities to connect and work with some of the best in the Canadian music business. That's where the big hitters were. So in the summer of 1985, we sold our home, took only what we could fit in our van, and moved out to the coast. As we were getting settled, we continued to play and travel as a duo for a few months before finding a management team that liked Carole's voice, her songwriting, and our drive. They recommended we form a band, so throughout the winter of 1985, we auditioned members. At that time, Vancouver and Toronto were the centers for music in Canada; consequently, there was a decent pool of musicians to choose from. By early January of 1986, we settled on a drummer, Rick, and another guitar player, Al, whose synth guitar would add variety and depth to our sound.

By that spring, we were ready to hit the road and start touring as a four-piece band. For the next two years, we played and toured across BC, Alberta, Saskatchewan, Manitoba, and the Northwest Territories. Over that time, we would replace our drummer and guitar player. The road can wear on you and it takes its toll on relationships, so it's normal to have to replace members. It makes it challenging though to establish a continuity of sound. Whenever we were home, we would find time to get into a local recording studio and lay some tracks of Carole's songs that we'd been working up on the road. From those recordings, we were able to get airplay in some of the smaller US, Canadian, and European markets, but we had a long way to go.

We thought it was a start, but in the end, nothing substantial came of it. Every so often over these years, thanks to our management team, we'd get the opportunity to play some local high-profile summer festivals and open some concert dates for high-profile acts such as Waylon Jennings, Prairie Oyster, and B.J. Thomas. We continued to tour for the next year and achieved occasional moments of success, but nothing that created any serious traction for us. In November of 1987, we had our third child, Robert. Kat was now school age; it was becoming increasingly difficult to manage the band and our family, and ensure that Kat had her education needs properly attended to.

By the time 1988 rolled around, it was clear from both a financial and emotional perspective that there was a heavy toll being exacted on everyone. It was becoming increasingly challenging to keep it all going. The touring was wearing on Carole in a big way—trying to be a performer at night and a mother and school teacher by day, since the kids were still travelling with us. We were unable to take time off simply because we couldn't afford to. Kat was now six, Robyn three, and Robert was just a baby. There were bills to pay, a home to support, and we had members who like us were depending on work to pay their bills. We simply had to keep working to keep the band together. We were not close to the caliber to command big paydays and that reality was slipping further away. Although I sensed it at the time, I refused to accept it. The only thing I understood was that if we had a chance of making it, we had to keep going. If nothing else, I am a glutton for punishment—not to mention stubborn. I was so intent on pursuing this career course that I continued to persist through it all without giving much serious thought to the state of our finances or the impact it was having on my family. I kept thinking about creating that one big chance, one big payday that would put us over the top and solve all our problems. Did I mention I can also be naïve? I was so determined that we had what it took to be successful that I failed to see the signposts for the emotional and financial brick wall we were heading for. Once Kat hit school age, the die was cast, even though for the next two years Carole (the trooper that she is) would school our daughter on the road, getting her through grades one and two. But with the added stress on her already overloaded plate, we were eventually forced to make other arrangements for our children. We arranged to have them stay at home while we were on the road. We continued to tour for the next two years, but in 1990 we made the decision to pull the band off the road and work on recording and playing locally. Over that time, I continued to work with our management company to put us in a situation where we might catch a break. Even then the writing was on the wall, but I still didn't want to see it. For the next five years, we continued to play in and around town and just across the line in Northern Washington. But in the winter of 1995, reality came knocking with a sledgehammer. We couldn't keep going, either from a financial or emotional perspective. The time had come to put the dream down—it was over. I was forty-eight and Carole was thirty-five; in the music business, you're done if you haven't established yourself by then. Music, as with many things in our culture, is all about youth. I was well past mine and Carole, with her beautiful voice and songwriting, wasn't enough to carry us. I may have started playing in my mid-twenties, but I wasn't there any longer.

In the moments when I've looked back at that time in my life, I've come to realize just how naïve and immature I was in my arrogant ignorance. How merciless I was in pushing Carole, and eventually the band, in the pursuit of my dream. For a time I was willing to sacrifice everything to find that elusive thing called success, but in the end, I would not sacrifice my family.

As the dust began settling from the decision to put down my dream, a new reality raised its head: insolvency. Throughout the fall of 1995, I did what I could to assimilate our debt to make it more manageable, but to no avail. In January of 1996, Carole and I made the decision to declare bankruptcy. That's when I knew my dream was truly over. That decision became the last nail in the coffin of my music career. My future of playing music professionally until I passed away was done. I was now just another washed up ex-musician. I was embarrassed and ashamed—no one likes to admit failure.

Now what? What was I going to do? I didn't have a clue. There had never been a Plan B. With my dream lying shattered around my feet, I felt like I was walking in a nightmare from which I couldn't wake up. All I'd known for the past twenty-plus years was playing, singing, promoting, and travelling. I loved my family more than anything—even though at that time I did not show them that love anywhere near as much as I could have—how was I going to protect and care for them? The only way I'd known was gone and I had no other skills to speak of. It would be hard to find a decent paying job; I had nothing to offer an employer other than brute labor. I was lost with no direction home, as Bob Dylan would say.

When we'd pulled the band off the road and began working locally, Carole was able to find stable employment, but the income wasn't enough to pay our living expenses and the band's bills. She would work during the day and we'd play on the weekends while I did what I could to move the band forward. All the years of travelling, equipment, recording, vehicles, loans, and more had become a weight on our shoulders, and we were sinking under it. We had accrued enough debt that, with the income we were bringing in, it would take decades to pay it all off, so we made the decision to wipe the slate clean and start over. We'd declare bankruptcy and moved on with our lives.

By August of 1996, we were slowly working our way through the bankruptcy process. We learned to live a cash-only life. I will always remember it, but I never want to repeat it. The bitterness and anger for me was palpable. I truly felt I had been cheated, but the worst of it all was that I felt defeated. When I first started playing music back in the seventies, I had made a commitment to myself that music would not only be a career for me but also a way of life. I believed in the power of music as one of the purest forms of human communication. I believed that people's lives could be enriched and changed through song. I had dedicated myself to creating a life in music. I believed I had done everything in my power to achieve that goal and that success was always just around the corner. I thought I had earnestly worked for it. But in the end, I was wrong, and now I was looking for something to live for again.

Our friend Bruce had been the drummer in our band for the past few years and in 1995 he started training in taekwondo at a local do-jahng. As he progressed through the art, he began sharing with us some of the positive changes he was experiencing. Carole and I noticed some of those changes as well. He became calmer, more focused, and happier. I think Carole was hoping the same thing might happen for me. I have never been an easy man to live with—at times volatile, and at others moody—and during this time I was worse. She has told me over the years that she hoped it might bring some positive influences back into my life. I had become a mess physically, mentally, and emotionally, but I continually resisted going to a class with whatever excuse popped into my mind. When we're in a bad place, even what's good can look bad.

Over the years, I've come to realize some of my reticence stemmed from growing up in the sixties. I remember in junior high (grades 7–9) that the kids we most feared at school were the ones who took martial arts training. I still remember their names to this day.

"When we're in a bad place, even what's good can look bad"

They were the ones always picking fights, apparently to practice their techniques and show off their developing skills. To me and others, they were just bullies. In the back of my mind, it didn't matter what positive changes Bruce was experiencing; the last thing I wanted to do was associate myself with martial arts and the thought of violence. I was already angry enough and I could not see how going to a class and learning how to kick and punch was going to make me feel any better. What happened to change my mind and make me go that one day in August of 1996? I don't know, other than that the club Bruce recommended was quite a bit closer to our home than where he normally trained. For whatever reason, that seemed to make a difference and my resistance weakened. I relented. In hindsight, it may have simply been that I wanted to do something physical again. It had been thirty years or more since I'd done anything with my body besides yoga.

I had no idea what to expect from that first class. I had been to a couple of Bruce's tests, where I watched the students demonstrate their form, do some sparring, and break boards. I didn't know what I was in for other than that there would be some physical activity and I'd be doing something with my body. I may have been hoping for some kind of a physical and emotional release to help exorcise the pent-up tension, anger, and frustration I was living with daily. I thought I might enjoy hitting the bags; it could be a stress release and maybe for a moment I could forget my sense of failure. I took that first step and went to class, and I never looked back.

On stage at the Merritt Mountain Music Festival

Lorne and Carole promotional shot

MASTER LORNE DAVIDSON

Lorne and Carole with Silver City

CHAPTER 2
CLASSES, LEARNING, AND TESTING

"I can do all things through Christ who strengthens me"
—*Philippians 4:13*

Class that day was run by a young man in his mid-twenties—almost half my age. Everyone called him Mr. Ford or sir, and I was attending his club. He remains my instructor to this day. He was a cheerful, welcoming young man, as were all the students in the club, but I felt awkward and out of place. Over my years of training and instructing, I have come to realize that every new student feels the same way when they attend their first martial arts class, regardless of age. In class that night, I was by far the oldest person by a good twenty years, which you can imagine only added to my sense of discomfort. However, it was enjoyable and there were a lot of good positive interactions and energy. We were to refer to the instructor as either sir, mister, or ma'am. That day I learned a lesson in humility: having to call someone half my age sir or mister can be a bit disconcerting. Going from a world where everything was casual and offhand into a life of protocol, formality, and discipline was challenging at first. After a few lessons though, it became more comfortable and, yes, to this

> **"That day I learned a lesson in humility: having to call someone half my age sir or mister can be a bit disconcerting"**

day I still call him Sir or Mr. Ford, even twenty years later. He is now Senior Master Ford, and I would never think to call him by his given name.

My first class went okay. The mental concepts and physical movements were completely foreign to me, having been raised on the traditional North American sports of hockey, soccer, baseball, and football. But there was definitely a physical release and enjoyment that came with the physical and mental discipline. In fact, I enjoyed the class enough that I went back for a second one. At the time, I had no idea what it was about the training that was helping improve my mood and demeanor. Over the intervening years, I've learned from my studies in fitness that, when we work out, two hormones are released into our bloodstream. The first are endorphins, which are released to help mask the pain and discomfort of physical exertion. The second is dopamine, which makes us feel good when we accomplish something. Starting to feel it, I went back for my third class. Something was starting to change in me that I couldn't quite put my finger on. I may have been hesitant about going to class, but after training I always felt great coming home. Why was that?

All the classes were held in a church two days a week. There was anywhere from ten to twenty students in a class, ranging from age seven to me, the older guy. Mr. Ford was an energetic and motivating instructor, and he kept us all engaged and actively participating. I enjoyed feeling accepted by the other students, even as a white belt. As an instructor, Mr. Ford was fun but firm and he built a supportive family atmosphere. I believe his approach helped me lay the groundwork for my schools—but I'll get to that later. After my third lesson, I had to decide if I was going to continue or gracefully bow out. If I chose to sign up and continue, I would have to commit to three months with a uniform for $150. That seemed straightforward enough, but when you're working your way out of bankruptcy, it's a lot of money. It's money that could be spent on groceries, kids' clothing, and gas for the car, but Carole encouraged me to enroll and keep going. She wanted me to sign up, assuring me that we would find the money somewhere, which we did. That was how my journey started.

MASTERSHIP

Our training consisted of the physical training—Songahm Taekwondo—and the mental/emotional training, which we called life skills. Over every testing cycle, the students would study one-word concepts such as courtesy, respect, and loyalty (to name a few). Testing cycles were either eight or nine weeks long and we studied the skill through quotes and proverbs from the Bible. This skill would be incorporated into as many aspects of our class training as possible. We learned how to demonstrate courtesy when dealing with a fellow student; how to be respectful to one's parents, husband, or wife simply by being aware of the tone in our voice when speaking with them; and how to demonstrate loyalty to the things we had committed to. We were encouraged to memorize one of the quotes or proverbs to help us incorporate this skill into our everyday lives. When it came time to test, we would relate how our quote had helped us gain a better understanding of that cycle's life skill and how we had worked to weave it into our lives outside of the club.

In my training as a white belt, I chose the proverb from Philippians 4:13: "I can do all things through Christ who strengthens me." It resonated with me, and I felt stronger inside whenever I read it. Although I had not been to church for over forty years, I still believed in God and Christ. At that time though, I simply needed to find something inspirational to help me develop some internal strength, and this proverb helped. Over my years of training that verse has remained with me and has become a part of my everyday life through my daily morning meditations. Throughout all my disappointments, challenges, and successes, it has helped keep me grounded, focused, and connected to the first steps that led into my second life. Over the past years, this proverb has become my gauge for helping me assess my actions. If my actions were in alignment with the teachings of Christ, I felt a certainty of success.

Once I made the financial and emotional commitment to train for the next three months, I promised myself I'd begin training at home as well. At that time, we were renting a three-bedroom house with a two-car garage, which was to become a great space to work out in. I cleaned it up and organized it, putting some old carpet down, and began working out on a daily basis. I decided that, if I was going to spend good money to do this, then I was going to put the effort in and get my money's worth. I would be all in. Being the oldest student in the club, I wanted to set a good example for myself and the other students. As well, I wanted to acquit myself of my past mistakes, old beliefs and habits. I was going to strive to be the best and train to be in the best shape possible. I still train at least four days a week for a minimum of one hour, over and above the hours I spend on the mats teaching and demonstrating. I joke with our students now that they are just training in my glorified garage, as all I did was exchange the carpets for mats.

As I worked my way through the three-month trial period, Mr. Ford encouraged me to test in November. Even though I was enjoying the training, I didn't feel confident enough in my skills to test. However, in January of 1997 at the age of forty-nine, I successfully tested for my orange belt and, in March of 1998, for my yellow belt. Ever so gradually, a growing sense of confidence and accomplishment was developing; it was something I hadn't experienced for many years. I started to think about where I wanted to go from there.

It was early June of 1997. I had arranged to meet with Mr. Ford at a local coffee shop to review my progress. My three months had come and gone, and we had worked out an arrangement that allowed me to continue my training in the basics program. However, it was time to discuss taking the next step into the black belt training program. Mr. Ford was interested to find out what benefits I had experienced from the last nine months of training. He also wanted to know how serious I was about taking my training to the next level. Even though I had been in the club for close to a year, I found it hard to articulate the benefits I was experiencing. I was aware that I felt better mentally, physically, and emotionally, but those feeling were inconsistent, even with my improving sense of accomplishment and calm. At home there was a growing sense of stability developing that, combined with a strengthening confidence, brought some peace to my life and to my family's.

Was I enjoying the training? Yes. It gave me something positive to look forward to and focus on for two days every week. It also gave me some genuine physical and emotional relief from the frustration and disappointment of the past few years. As with anything though, it takes time to understand the cumulative benefits. At that moment, it was challenging to articulate the effects. I didn't understand the subtle effects my training was having on my thoughts and actions, but it was there; it felt like a tickle in the back of my mind.

Mr. Ford was also curious to know what plans I had for my taekwondo training and future. We had gotten to know each other over the last few months and he had learned a bit about my history. He was interested to know where I saw myself going in this world of Songahm Taekwondo. He was a bit taken aback when I told him I had spent some time thinking about the results of testing regularly for the next twenty years. I asked him if I understood things correctly—if I continued training regularly, maintained my health, and tested consistently, I could test for my sixth degree in my sixty-ninth year, with the possibility of becoming a Master by the time I was seventy. He looked at me and said that seemed plausible.

Looking back, I don't recall where the idea to do that research came from or why I took the time to figure it all through, but I did. After our talk though, I promptly forgot all about it, but unknowingly I had planted a seed. I started doing something I'd never consciously done before and certainly didn't realize I was doing at the time—I was setting a long-term goal, one that would take twenty years. I had done similar things with music, but in all those dreams, there were no benchmarks or deadlines. There was nothing to aim at, just a vague nebulous dream of future success somewhere down the road. At that time, as odd as it may sound, I had no definitive concept of goal setting.

During our conversation, Mr. Ford mentioned that when I joined the club my goal was to become a black belt, right! I replied, "No, I'd just wanted to see if I could successfully test to my orange belt and then I'll think about yellow." In my reality at the time, I had no idea of anything longer than a month or two; it was a hangover from my previous life. The idea of earning my black belt was not even a glimmer on the horizon. Projecting where I could be in twenty years had been a fun exercise, but that was it. I soon found out that exercises, both mental and physical, can develop into tangible results.

In May of 1997, I'd successfully tested for my camouflage belt; that's what precipitated the meeting with Mr. Ford. This put me about two and a half years away from achieving that black belt if I successfully passed all my tests. I was eighteen and a half years away from my sixth degree (with another year of training just for good measure) to become a Master. At that time in our style of taekwondo, when a student received their camouflage belt, they moved from the basics program into the black belt training program. That required them to make a commitment to continue their training and work towards achieving their black belt. One of the new requirement at camouflage belt is the student must spar to be able to progress in rank.

I wasn't too keen on the idea of sparring for a couple of reasons. First, I've never been much of a physical fighter. When I was younger, whenever I got into a scrap, I was usually on the losing end. I'd learned to fight with my mind more than my body and I shied away from physical confrontation. Second, it would mean another expense for protective sparring gear. In Songahm, other than the instructors, everyone has to go to school or work the next day so safety is essential when making contact—and in sparring contact will be made. Protective head, hand, and foot gear were mandatory, along with mouth guards and cups for men. Sparring was one of the requirements as set out by our organization and, if I was going to continue, I would have to overcome both obstacles. Sparring has never been my favorite discipline. Forms, board breaking, and weapons training bring me more satisfaction. Maybe it reminds me of the kids who studied martial arts back in the sixties who liked to pick fights. I don't know. Like it or not, it was a requirement to test and part of our class training, so it had to become part of my everyday regimen. Even though it was not something I looked forward to, the discipline of sparring taught me some valuable lessons about myself and life in general.

"The discipline of sparring taught me some valuable lessons about myself and life in general"

I have never forgotten a lesson from early in my sparring development. During one of my first sparring classes, I was with one of the club's senior red/black belts. At that time, I weighed about 140 pounds soaking wet and my opponent was a much bigger and younger man. He was in his mid-twenties and weighed in at around 210 pounds. As we were sparring, he executed a beautiful spin hook kick and caught me with some force on the side of the head. It was the first time I'd been hit hard in the head in a long time. It rattled my brain and I didn't much like it. In fact, I was mad and embarrassed. I stomped around the training floor for a few seconds, trying to regain my bearings and muttering some inappropriate words under my breath. Mr. Ford quickly came over to check on me and helped calm me down. After a few minutes, I was able to regain my composure. I got back to the match, though inside I was still seething. I went looking for a chance to even the score and sure enough it came.

Have you ever noticed that, when you're looking for something, it tends to show up? I saw an opening and punched him hard in the chest. It was hard enough that I knocked him back a couple of steps, which for the moment made me feel a little better. I felt I had redeemed myself. Later though, I would come to regret my actions, but that night I felt I had stood up for myself. Soon the match ended, and we shook hands and moved on to the next match.

For the next two weeks, I noticed this student wasn't in class. The club wasn't that big so, when someone wasn't there, it was noticeable. When I saw him again, I made a point of going over to ask where he'd been and to let him know he'd been missed. His reply taught me the lesson of self-control and how my lack of it had negatively affected him. He said, "A guy about your size hit me pretty hard in the chest one night while sparring.

> **"In victory be humble, in defeat be strong, in all things be fair."**
> **—Eternal Grand Master H.U. Lee**

It was hard enough that for three days I had trouble breathing and couldn't go to work. It's just now I'm finally able to get back to class because I can breathe normally again without my chest hurting." I knew he was talking about me and I felt terrible knowing that my lack of physical and emotional control had hurt someone. I felt humbled and ashamed. I apologized to him and we shook hands.

MASTER LORNE DAVIDSON

I have never forgotten that experience or the lesson. Now, many years later, I have had a lot of sparring experiences, but no matter what happens in the ring, my response is always tempered with physical and emotional control. A quote from Eternal Grand Master said it best for me: "In victory be humble, in defeat be strong, in all things be fair."

The second valuable lesson came from my early sparring matches as well. This one focuses on our ability to use our minds to overcome pain, whether physical or mental. When necessity meets obligation, by using self discipline we have the ability to overcome any pain or obstacle.

On those nights when I was learning how to spar, I would inevitably end up clashing shins with my opponent. This was due to my lack of experience and discipline. I was doing nothing more than reacting to my opponent's action with an identical action, which in these particular cases was usually a round kick. Two of us would be sparring and my opponent would attack with a back leg round kick. Seeing this, I would counter with a back leg round kick of my own. Somewhere in the middle of those two kicks, our shins would meet, usually quite forcefully and painfully. After a few rounds of sparring with shin clashes, I'd be in fair amount of pain.

Many nights I wondered when I was going to learn to be more disciplined and stop reacting to someone else's actions. It became most challenging on the nights when I had to deliver papers after training. At that time I drove a little standard shift four speed Toyota. I'd drive to the drop point, which didn't give me the option of resting my banged-up leg. I'd get the papers and drive and walk the route for about three hours. Those nights were difficult.

When we declared bankruptcy, I wasn't trained for much that could help with the family's finances. One of the only options was delivering papers at night, so I took it. At forty-nine and having been a musician for the last twenty-odd years, I hadn't developed much that would look good on a résumé. To start applying for a job at my age with no current skills didn't give me much confidence, so I did what I could. I delivered papers at night while Carole worked days. The nights after sparring, I often had to pick myself up off the couch, get in my car,

MASTERSHIP

and drive. If you have ever had to do a lot of walking on sore, bruised shins, you'll know that this was not something I looked forward to—nor was it particularly easy. Yet I learned that, by not giving into the pain, I could overcome it. I learned to do what I came to call "walking over the pain." Even though it was incredibly sore at the beginning of the route, by the time I finished three hours later, the pain would be significantly less, and my legs and body a lot more comfortable. I would be left with the satisfaction of having done my job while not giving into the pain. I began to realize how powerful the mind is in helping overcome whatever obstacle one may face.

Over time, and with the responsibility of contributing to the family's bottom line, I eventually learned to discipline myself into not reacting to someone's kick. As our Grand Master Emeritus Soon Ho Lee says, "There is always more to learn."

To that end, here is an essay I read in 2001 in *Black Belt Magazine* by Richard McClain. It speaks to the concept of "mind over matter."

> *During Korea's Silla Dynasty (57 BC–935 AD) a famous monk named Won Hyo Daesa decided to embark on a pilgrimage to India. One night while he was on the road, a storm rolled in and obscured the light of the moon, making the countryside dark and travel dangerous. Rain poured down and the wind blew furiously.*
>
> *Won Hyo Daesa searched frantically for shelter from the storm. He stumbled upon a small, dry cave and crawled inside; it was so dark he had to use his hands to find his way. The floor felt as though it was padded with straw. He thought this was wonderful as he was quite tired from the journey. Now he not only had a dry place to sleep but a comfortable one. Won Hyo Daesa lay down and pondered the good sleep he would have.*
>
> *The hypnotic rainfall and hours of walking began to take their toll and he fell fast asleep. Later he awoke with a terrific thirst and after feeling around in the darkness he*

found a cup with water in it. How wonderful, he thought, not only did he have a dry place to sleep but he also had water to quench his thirst. He drank the water then laid back down to finish his sleep.

When morning came the monk woke up, stretched, and thought about his good fortune the night before. As his eyes adjusted to the light, he gazed around and was shocked by what he saw. His shelter was actually a tomb with bones strewn about the floor. Looking down he found the cup he drank from was actually part of a human skull with old stagnant water inside. Upon realizing this, he became ill and staggered to a corner to be sick.

Afterwards he meditated on the events that had occurred the night before and the following morning. Won Hyo Daesa concluded that nothing could harm him unless he allowed it to. When he thought everything was wonderful, he was physically, mentally, and spiritually comfortable even after drinking the stagnant water. It was only after his mind and body reacted to his perception of the events and surroundings that he became ill.

Won Hyo Daesa's lesson is as valuable today as it was to him. If someone gives you a dirty look or shouts a foul word in your direction, it cannot affect you unless you let it. The mind ultimately controls the body, for example some people become excited, nervous, sick, or worried when they are confronted with a problem. These reactions are more and more leading to health, financial, and family problems and breakdowns. We can protect ourselves by building a strong mind, which in Korean is called saeng hwal mu do (life style martial arts).

The physical benefits of martial arts are obvious but pale in comparison to the mental and spiritual rewards that come from increased confidence, humility, and focus. These attributes allow us to defend ourselves against the mental enemies of stress, worry, and fear. As Won Hyo Daesa learned during his journey, mental enemies are just as real and dangerous as any physical foe. Treating your art as "saeng hwal mu do" can prepare you for not only physical dangers but for the ever so prevalent mental dangers as well.

The moral of this story is something I carry with me every day. Simply put, we must feed our minds with the best fuel or our minds will feed us whatever it happens to run across. I learned that self-control is not just a physical act, but also a mental discipline.

At the age of fifty-one, after nearly three years of training, in 1999 I tested for my first degree black belt. It was a bright, sunny Saturday morning and believe me when I say I was as nervous as I'd ever been. Once the testing began, I was able to settle in. I was on the floor from the start of testing to the end. I had to successfully demonstrate all nine color belt forms (white through red), spar three rounds, demonstrate my self-defense skills, and finish by breaking boards.

The testing was two hours of constant mental and physical challenges, but I made it. Afterwards, I was exhausted. It would take a few weeks before I found out I had passed; it was one of the proudest days of my life.

At a tournament shortly after receiving my first degree, not yet in the leadership program

Carole, Robert, Robyn, and me at the Gateway club

MASTERSHIP

Gateway club, just received my red collar

Robert and me in Oahu, Hawaii, visiting my mom

CHAPTER 3
BECOMING AN INSTRUCTOR AND CLUB OWNER

"Choose a job you love and you will never work a day in your life."

—*Confucius*

That Saturday in May of 1999, when I successfully tested and achieved my first degree black belt, I thought back to the discussion I'd had with Mr. Ford in May of 1997. Back then, this reality had not been on my radar. My goal of reaching sixth degree by my seventieth birthday was something I'd never fully conceived of until that moment. I had simply been enjoying the process. Never had I fully realized that to get to that theoretical goal of Mastership, I would have to go through this day, as well as the second, third, fourth, and fifth degree black belt rank testing, and the numerous mid-terms per belt rank that are required. I'd simply found pleasure and purpose in the training. Every time I passed a test, I moved onto the next challenge. The concept of goal setting was not fully formed within me yet, but that was all about to change.

Over those three years, we'd worked ourselves clear of the bankruptcy process; learning how to manage our household on a cash-only basis was challenging. There was certainly less stress as there were no major bills hanging over our heads. But it was more restrictive simply because there wasn't much extra cash to go around. The lessons I learned then stay with me to this day.

Attaining my first degree belt brought about another decision—I now had a choice of either joining the leadership program with the goal of becoming an instructor or simply remaining a student and continue training. If I remained a student, nothing would change financially and I could continue to train, which I enjoyed. I could still be delivering papers years later and, as time would tell; there was no future in that occupation. I wasn't getting any younger—in August of that year I had turned fifty-two. I needed a future. I may have been in my fifties, but I wasn't old. Joining the leadership program could give me the opportunity to create that future and potentially work to become a certified instructor. This would not only give me a recognized certification within our organization, but also allow me the option of opening my own school or working for another school owner. Achieving certified instructor status would also give me the opportunity to share my knowledge and life experience with other students, old and young alike, along with their families.

"With every opportunity, there is always a cost attached"

I was beginning to realize that with every opportunity, there is always a cost attached. If I chose to pursue the leadership certification process, we would again be challenged financially. We would not only be required to pay more on a monthly basis, but there would be the extra cost involved of attending the necessary seminars to attain the certification. There would be travel expenses like hotels, gas, and meals involved in getting to and from many of the seminars.

Having invested the time, energy, and money in my training, becoming part of the leadership program seemed to be the next logical step. It was a step I truly thought necessary. Now the challenge became how to make it happen.

Going bankrupt at forty-eight (or at any age) is not the way anyone envisions them self ending up. To start over again, we'd made a clean break from the past and were now moving on. At fifty-two, four years out and having stepped away from my previous career, I was working hard to re-envision my life. Joining this program might give me the opportunity to do just that. In the beginning, I hadn't seen martial arts training as a way of starting over; it was just a way to physically and mentally work my way through the bitterness, frustration, and disappointment of the past twenty years. Over the course of the three years from 1996 to 1999, I began to see that maybe there was a way for me to start over. There was a glimmer of hope. Something in what I was learning about myself through my training in the arts held the promise of something better. However, to make that happen, many things would have to fall into place at the right time. As well, some things would need to be accomplished before that possibility could even become more than just a hope.

Looking back on it now, it's hard for me to understand how and why I was as fortunate as I was; I just know now I was. The big things and decisions are easy for me to remember and understand. It's the little ones that can cause the whole fabric to unravel. These are the ones that I feel the most fortunate for. Somehow, when those opportunities were presented I was guided to make the correct choices. I had help from that still small voice within me and those close to me whose council I listened to. I trusted the ones whose love and support I had, my family, friends, and the encouragement and direction of my instructor.

During those three plus years, something was reawakened in me by the training, something that my heart and mind had been trying to bring to my attention for many years. They were thoughts and feelings that I had been consistently pushing away, ignoring, and willing to sacrifice in my stubborn resolve to become successful in music, even as I continued to put my family deeper into financial trouble. Reawakened were life concepts—the way to live that had been instilled in me by my mother as I was growing up, but which over the years I had forgotten and just plain ignored in my impatient rush to become successful in the music business.

In the *do-jahng* (Korean for taekwondo facility), we referred to these concepts as our life skills. These include concepts and understandings like courtesy, respect, loyalty, and self-control. Over these past years of training, I had been reminded and reintroduced to concepts my mother had taught me so many years earlier. During my time in training, it became obvious to me just how much I had strayed from and been missing those qualities in my everyday life for many years. The more I trained and studied, the more I realized I wanted to re-establish them in my life. I wanted to regain my health. I also began to think that these life skills might be something worth sharing with others. If I was feeling a lack of these influences in my life with all the stress and pressure of everyday living, I was confident that I wasn't the only one who might benefit from them. The possibility of becoming an instructor would not only be a way to help myself, but I would be putting myself in a position to help others. For now though, the first step was to join the leadership program.

It would give me the opportunity to start assisting in class. This would be the starting point to help me develop the necessary skills to become a quality instructor. It would also give me the opportunity to share some of my personal experiences with others. To be able to share something, we need a root to hold us firm. For me, that root was quickly becoming Songahm Taekwondo. From the position of instructor, I could not only share my experiences, but also the values and benefits I had found in my training. Hopefully by sharing some of my personal stories and how taekwondo had changed my life, I could inspire others to their own possibilities. The only way for me to become that instructor was through the leadership program. It was the next step and one I had to take no matter what the cost.

To become a certified instructor was and still is a lengthy process. It can be compared to earning a BA degree. In fact, my instructor Senior Master Ford has a BA, and another local instructor I know received an MA. Both told me a few times that the education they received going through the instructor certification process was more valuable to them than the education they received at university. When I started the program, the trainees needed to accumulate three hundred volunteer teaching hours as part of their requirements.

I was to get my first hour of instructing shortly after receiving my red collar instructor uniform. Walking into class to train one night, Mr. Ford said, "You've got the class tonight. It's yours to run." I was

MASTERSHIP

dumbstruck. I'd never even run a warm up before and now my instructor wanted me to teach an hour long class to all ranks. Yikes. Thankfully there were other trainees there for help, support, and encouragement. They told me throughout the class that they had experienced a similar fate. Having a class plan and their help made the class manageable. I had stood on many stages in my music career, but this was a stage I had no preparation for. That night I sweated bullets, but I made it through with the help of the other senior rank trainees, earning my first volunteer hour and receiving my baptism by fire on my journey to becoming an instructor.

Volunteer hours were one of two requirements for a trainee to be eligible to obtain certification. These hours could be accomplished within one's own school or club, or at other affiliate schools by teaching or assisting in their classes. The second requirement was to attend and pass seven specific all-weekend seminars designed to develop and educate us to be the best instructor possible. These seminars consisted of the history of taekwondo, testing procedures, curriculum management, tiny tigers (ages 4–6), karate for kids (ages 7–13), adult training (14 and up), and class management skills. Once the three hundred hours had been achieved and we'd attended and passed the seminar requirements, we would then attend a final certification seminar to test in front of a panel of Master Instructors.

"That was then this is now; I would never know the result until I took action"

As with every decision along this journey, I was continually assailed by doubts about my abilities. I was pretty confident I could handle the teaching end of things, but I hadn't been in a situation where I would be required to pass a test in thirty-some-odd years. I had no idea how I was going to handle that part of the training. Even though the seminars would only be held over a weekend with months in between each one, I was still nervous. I did not have fond memories of my school years. The answer that came to me from that still small voice inside me was "that was then this is now, and you'll never know until you step into the room." I would never know the result until I took action.

It has been said that, if there is a perceived value in something, then people will pay whatever is necessary. This was the case with our family and my continued training in Songahm Taekwondo. In 1997, we enrolled our son in the club because he was being bullied regularly at school. Carole joined in January of 1999 and for a short period our two daughters trained as well. To our family, the benefits of the training were evident and everyone got involved. With Mr. Ford's help and understanding, we arranged a special family training rate to be able to pay our monthly dues and testing fees. With me looking at taking this step, we would once again have to sit down and crunch the numbers.

In the three years since we'd declared bankruptcy, we had become more conscious of where the money was, where it was going, and how much we had to spend. During that time, I was able to sign up for a credit card with a low limit, and we decided we could use it to register for the necessary seminars online and then pay it off before taking the next seminar. The next step was to discuss with Mr. Ford what our payment arrangements would be. Once these steps were completed to everyone's satisfaction, I joined the leadership program in September of 1999.

In the fall of 1999, at fifty-two years of age, there appeared to be a future developing in front of me. I began to feel hopeful again. As a member of the club's leadership program, I was about to embark on a potential new career. The first seminar was on December 4, leaving little time to think about it. It was time to jump into the deep end of the pool.

I'd always had dreams and made plans for a great many things, some of which I'd been able to achieve, but the results had been inconsistent at best. That was all about to change.

My introduction to the power and benefit of writing my dreams and plans down as a series of goals came one night in September of 1999 in one of my first leadership classes. Mr. Ford asked all of us to do something I had never done before—write down five goals. In fifty-two years, I had never done that before. I remember just sitting there for a few moments. Where do I begin? What are my goals? To earn a better living? Everyone wants that. Could that be considered a goal? To become an instructor? Sure, hopefully, but in reality, what are the odds? To own a school? Now that's stretching it. What are the chances of that ever happening? Many thoughts ran through my mind about what I could write down. As soon as I had a thought, others would come in and shoot it down. My thoughts became like a dog chasing its tail, going around in circles.

After a few anxious moments, I calmed down enough to write down some thoughts: "To become a certified instructor" and "To own a martial arts school." I wrote those two down because they were the two things that were staring me in the face and they were the reason I was in the leadership program to begin with. I also wrote them down out of sheer desperation just to have something.

That's a night I will never forget. That simple exercise was to change my life. By writing those two goals down, I would over the next three years learn just how powerful that act was. The power of what can happen when one puts a dream, an idea, no matter how far-fetched it seems, down on a piece of paper can be life changing. It set a target in front of me.

As soon as I wrote them down, all the negative thoughts came out of me: "Ya right, how are you ever going to do that? You're not smart enough! Who do you think you are? You're an old man, washed up! You're just clear of bankruptcy; you hardly have enough money to get by!" The thoughts went on and on, but somehow I was able to stay with what I had written. When Mr. Ford asked me what I had written, that's what I told him. I then put that piece of paper in my binder and forgot about it. Class was over, the exercise complete.

I may have written my goals down in desperation, but deep down they were what I wanted to do. If I had a chance of making a better life for myself and my family, it was through becoming an instructor and one day owning a school. I knew having joined the leadership program that I was taking a risk. I would be putting myself out there again and making a commitment to work for it. I also knew myself well enough to know that I would take whatever steps I could to be successful. I had pursued a career in music for twenty years; I just hoped this endeavor would be more successful. I would use whatever resources I had to put myself in the best position possible to one day accomplish the goal of becoming an instructor. After that, I'd look at the potential of owning my own school.

Did I have my doubts? Absolutely. The most obvious was wondering if I was up to entering the classroom again. Could I follow through for the next three years and become an instructor? After that, how does one open a school and successfully start a business?

You may ask what writing down a goal does for us. That's a great question and my answer would be this: It can plant a seed. It gives us a target, something to aim for. I wrote down three other things that night as well. I don't recall what they were, and I don't have the paper I wrote them on so I can't tell you how many of the five I accomplished, but I did succeed with two of them in a big way.

Every game I played as a kid—hockey, soccer, baseball, football—had the concept of a goal inherent in them. There would be no focus or purpose to the games if there wasn't a net, a base or a goal line, a result, something to aim for. Basketball wouldn't be basketball without a basket, would it? It's funny how the purpose of the sports we learn to play as we are growing up are somehow not translated into our everyday lives. We are taught the rules of each game and what or where the goals of each are. We know what the result looks like, but somehow throughout our schooling, we are left on our own to figure out how these concepts can be applied to our everyday life. I know it was that way when I was in school. I know that there have been improvements in the education process, but I still see children and young people coming through our academies who are searching for an understanding, of what the potential is for writing down a goal or dream and what it can do for them.

Every January, I write out my goals for the year. I have four main areas of goal setting: personal, business, career, and philanthropy. Do I achieve them all? Not by a long shot, but I complete a lot more than if I didn't write them down. The ones I don't complete get transferred over to the next year. Starting in October of 1999, my goal was to begin working towards my certified instructor black collar, setting me up to hopefully one day open my own school.

MASTERSHIP

To become an instructor, I would need to focus on my three hundred volunteer hours and pass the prescribed seminars, the first of which would be in December of 1999. To achieve my required volunteer hours, I had to start attending every non-training class possible. In the spring of 2000, I began assisting Mr. Ford in a small club he ran in the community of White Rock, BC. It is about thirty miles south of Vancouver on the border of Washington State. I assisted every Monday and Wednesday evening, delivered my papers at night, and trained every Tuesday and Thursday at the Gateway club. This routine was to become my new way of life—family, fitness, and martial arts. To be a creditable instructor, you have to be in shape, and one of the ways I worked to improve my conditioning and cardio was to run my paper route whenever I could. I'd simply park the car, grab a handful of papers, and go. I would challenge myself to finish the route in faster and faster times. I had a purpose and hope again.

The first seminar I attended in December of 1999 was held locally, so I was able to ease into this new world. Despite my nerves and concerns, I passed and took my first tentative step. In 2000, I was able to attend and passed three more (in June, August, and October). Things were looking promising and I was gradually moving closer to my first goal.

Over that year, Mr. Ford gave me the head instructor position at the White Rock club, as the Gateway club had continued to grow and it was taking more and more of his time. This definitely helped me with my volunteer hours and they began to accumulate rapidly. When I was assisting, I got a half-hour credit for every hour worked. Now I would get full credit for every hour worked.

By October of 2001, I had compiled over seven hundred volunteer hours and passed all seven of the required seminars for certification. Things were developing nicely. Now there was one more test left to pass, the certification seminar held on December 2, 2001. When that day came, there were six nervous trainee instructors all with a dream of becoming` certified instructors. The good thing was that we all knew each other as we had attended many of the same seminars over the last two plus years. We would be tested by the highest rank of instructors from the regions of BC and Washington State. The test was, if I remember correctly, about six hours in length, starting at ten in the morning and finishing around four. It was a grueling day, but I'm proud to say we all passed.

In February of 2002, at one of our regional tournaments, we were all officially presented with our black collar uniforms. I was now a second degree black belt certified instructor (I'd tested in December 2000 for my second degree). I had successfully achieved my first goal of becoming an instructor and had now been teaching on my own for almost a year, but all the hours were volunteer; I had not earned a penny.

I had barely enough time to get comfortable after achieving the first goal when Mr. Ford dropped a bombshell on me. Within months of receiving my black collar, he told me he was going to either sell the White Rock club to me or close it down. He and his wife had decided to move back to Edmonton to be closer to their families. For a moment, I didn't know what to say, I was in shock. First of all, I would be losing my instructor. From a student's perspective, this was disappointing enough, but the second thing for me personally was undoubtedly the most challenging. How was I possibly going to buy the White Rock club? I didn't have any magical savings to draw on. Yes, I had been running the club under his direction for over a year, but I was in no position to buy it. The proposition now was that I either had to commit to buying it or he was going to shut it down. I just stood there in silence, not knowing what to do or say. "Can I have some time to think about it?" I stammered. He graciously agreed and asked me to give him an answer as quickly as I could.

Wow, here it was, the opportunity and manifestation of another of the goals I had written down almost three years ago. Here was a chance to own and operate my own club. It was staring me in the face. Do you ever ask yourself why opportunities always seem to come up when it appears we are in no position to take advantage of them? That day I did. If I said yes, I would be taking a huge risk that I wasn't entirely sure I could live up to. I'd had no previous business experience. If I said no, would I be kicking myself years later because I let my doubts and fears get the better of me? Driving home that night, I thought about where I might be able to raise some money quickly and, if I could raise it, how I would pay it back. Nothing came to mind; I was drawing blanks. I couldn't think of any options. None of my friends had any money to speak of and I certainly couldn't go to a bank and apply for a loan. Also, I didn't have any idea how to successfully run a club. I had no previous business experience and certainly no background in it. All I'd ever been was a warehouseman and a touring musician.

I was now approaching my fifty-fifth birthday. Questions careened through my head: Could I learn to market and grow a school? How about managing the backend financials, order the needed inventory, and teach? How fast could I learn to do it? I certainly wasn't getting any younger. Where could I go to learn the ABCs of business, and if I learned them, how effectively could I apply them? For most of my life, I had been plagued with self-doubts. I felt as if I was standing on the edge of a cliff, knowing that if I said "yes" I would be taking a leap of faith. At that time, I didn't even know enough about business to ask questions like how much is the monthly income? How much do you pay for rent? What is the income from the testing? I had no one but Carole to turn to, no one to guide me or refer to.

Over the next few days, I did a lot of soul searching and Carole and I spent time talking it over. My decisions had not brought us a lot of success in the past, but we both agreed this was different. Carole encouraged me to seriously consider it. Throughout our twenty-one years of marriage, she had always supported me, right or wrong, and been there to hold me up when I faltered. Here she was, doing it again. One of her recommendations was that I contact Mr. Ford and find some time to talk with him. I needed to get a clearer picture of the details he had in mind for me purchasing the club and go from there. What was he was looking at pricewise and what was his idea on how we might structure the purchase? He knew I didn't have any available cash. Carole is a very smart woman; she's my heart and soul, and so that's precisely what I did.

The following week, I contacted Mr. Ford and let him know I was interested in purchasing the club. I asked him if we could get together as I needed some clarification on things like price and how the purchase could be structured. We would also have to inform headquarters about transferring the school into my name. When we met, he helped me deal with my doubts and concerns, and reassured me that I was more than capable of running the club on my own as I had been doing for the last year. He informed me of the rent he was paying and that I could pay for the school in little over a year by paying him the student testing fees I'd been collecting for him from the White Rock students. Testing was held every two months, which would mean six or seven payments, depending on how many students tested. We agreed that the White Rock students would test at the Gateway club in Surrey until he and Mrs. Ford decided to make their move to Edmonton. In this way, it would help both of us keep accurate figures on the monies being collected and paid. It was also an incentive for me to grow the school quickly, which is what I would set out to do. In the end, it came together rather easily. We came to an agreement and made up a document, which we both signed. Mr. Ford then notified HQ that he was selling me the club. This was the last step in moving it to my name and finalizing things with HQ. It took a couple of months, but in September of 2002, I officially became a club owner. I now owned school number 2196. Goal number two had been accomplished.

Wow, there were times I felt I was walking in a dream; those few months had brought me more success, accomplishment, and hope than I ever thought possible. Achieving certified instructor status and becoming a club owner all in one year—crazy. Only six years before I was a bankrupt musician. Now there was a future staring me in the face that I could never have imagined even in my wildest dreams. Talk about a rollercoaster ride; it was that and more, but the results spoke for themselves. There was a future calling me.

I had enrolled a few students over the year of teaching at the White Rock club, most by referral. There hadn't been a lot of incentive to push for more, other than having more students on the floor to teach, which always increases the energy in a class. It certainly didn't put any money in my pockets. Mr. Ford had never pushed me to enroll more students and honestly I never gave it a second thought. So, when I grasped the idea that the more students I enrolled, the more I'd help my bottom line, I took my first step into the world of business. The idea of paying off my debt quickly was very appealing. It didn't seem as scary as I had first thought. The rent was reasonable and was covered, if barely, by the existing students, so more on the floor meant more in the bank.

At the time I purchased the White Rock club, there were seven active students so I knew going in, if I wanted to pay off the club quicker, I had better get to work. Throughout it all, I felt good about the process and how it was unfolding. Ever so slowly, I was beginning to develop a stronger sense of self-confidence. I had a growing sense of achievement, even though I was still nervous. In all the twenty years I had played music, I'd never experienced anything close to this sense of achievement or accomplishment in such a short period. It was uplifting and I knew I had the ability to make it work. I willingly took on the challenge of growing the club, now my business, which held my future. I was confident that even though right now we only had seven students, I could make it grow. I was sure that the existing students would be more than willing to chip in.

One of the most satisfying days and gratifying moments to that point in my life was the night I walked into my club and got to tell the students that it was ours. I was not only their instructor, I owned the club, and we were going to make it grow. I can't begin to tell you what a tremendous sense of satisfaction that was. Somehow in the three years since writing down those two goals on a piece of paper, I was able to achieve both of them. Was I excited? Yes, but also humbled and a little scared. I was all those things and more, all at the same time. I had established a beachhead, a place from which to begin my new life. Here was my new starting point.

Carole, Robert, and me in our club

MASTERSHIP

My friend Bruce as a guest judge at one of our first testings

Friend and mentor Chris at our club's testing being a self-defense partner for one of our juniors

CHAPTER 4
A STARTING POINT

"Change is inevitable. Growth is optional."

—John Maxwell

Over my sixty-nine years, the hardest things I ever had to face down were my own fears. Whether they were rational or irrational, it didn't really matter. Throughout this journey however, I've come across two acronyms for fear that have helped me work through challenging times and give me a laugh at others. The first is: **F**alse **E**vidence **A**ppearing **R**eal. I can't count the number of times I've had fears that never even came close to becoming reality, but they made me doubt and second guess myself every time. The second acronym is when the fear is justified: **F***#% **E**verything **A**nd **R**un. My fears always stood in the way of my growth. As things changed around me, I had a tendency to hesitate. As the saying goes, "He who hesitates is lost." Throughout my life, I missed opportunities to grow and develop when I allowed my fear to get the better of me. The strength, both physical and mental, that I was developing through my training was allowing me to face the changes required and overcome my doubts and fears as I moved into this new life.

Fear—False Evidence Appearing Real

I was beginning to understand that many of my doubts and fears were created as much from my success and accomplishments as from perceived failures. Fear of messing it all up can be just as debilitating.

As the accomplishments of achieving my black belts, becoming a certified instructor, and now owning my club began to line up behind me, I began to feel the pressure. How do I keep this trend going? God, I hope I don't blow it. I was turning fifty-five; could I keep it up? The only thing I could think of to counter those ever-present fears was, believe it or not, to focus on giving the club a name. I wanted a name that would lay a solid foundation upon which to build, a name I could stand on. I wanted one that would represent what had been accomplished to date and carry my growing sense of achievement into the future. This name would not only be for me, but for all our students.

I couldn't keep the name Mr. Ford had for the club. I needed a completely separate identity, something new. I wanted a name that would communicate the fundamental reason for being in business. A name that would remind me every day what had been accomplished and what was yet to be. I needed to find something that would be as strong a reply to those doubts and fears as I could manifest. Even though it was only a name, it had to be something I could identify with. It would identify the culture and attitude that was to permeate the atmosphere inside the club and school to come. It would also speak to the ideal and attitude of what I hoped to develop in our students and parents. This attitude would be evident in the standard of their training on all levels—mental, physical, and emotional. At the time, I did not fully comprehend all this, but as we've successfully grown the business over the years, I've come to realize just what our name came to be. I believed firmly that the name would be crucial to our future success. It would be the foundation upon which our future students and instructors would grow.

Taekwondo is the martial art of Korea. General Hong Hi Choi created it to unify Korea shortly after the Korean War ended. I knew the name had to be Korean in origin. I wanted it to show respect to the Korean culture. Over the next couple of months, I came up with all kinds of concepts, but the only word that I kept coming back throughout was the English word "victory." It certainly expressed my journey to this point. It had been a continual series of small victories built one on top of another, much like the color belt system that takes a student from white to black. Victory also spoke to the purpose that I wanted to underlay our students' experience, not to mention the business as a whole. I believed this principle had to be something our future students and parents could relate to as well. Once I decided on this, I simply had to find the Korean word. I thought this would be the easiest part, but as with many things, there was a twist.

My son and I took the next step and went to the public library. It was easy to find an English/Korean dictionary, and we looked up the word that meant "victory." The word was *seung-ri*. It was simple. I liked it and that was that. Simple. Done. Although it had taken months of thought to articulate what I truly wanted in a name, the final decision took no more than an hour. In the late fall of 2002, I registered the name "Seung-ri Black Belt Academy" with the Canadian government and became an official business. I thought that was the end of it.

However, shortly after deciding on the name and getting it officially registered, Mr. Ford and I were talking. He asked me if I had picked a name for the club. I told him what it was and what it meant. He looked at me a little funny and said, "But I thought *pil-seung* meant 'victory.'" My heart sank. He was right, that's what Eternal Grand Master had always signed whenever he autographed anything for a student. He would always sign in Korean *pil-seung* and his name. Crap. Had I made a mistake? Had I misunderstood? What would I do now? I was bombarded with fear and concerns that somehow I'd messed up. I had to get this right as I'd already notified HQ and registered the name with the government. As soon as I could, I went back to the library to check but it still said that *seung-ri* was Korean for "victory." That was a relief. How was I going to get to the bottom of this? Where could I go to find the truth regarding the correct meaning of these two Korean words that both seemingly meant the same thing?

My answer was to come from one of our local Korean Masters. Shortly after talking with Mr. Ford, I was at one of our regional tournaments. While there, I had the opportunity to ask Master Cho about this apparent discrepancy between two Korean words. Very politely he told me that both were correct. In the Korean language, *pil-seung* means "to strive for victory" and *seung-ri* means "victory achieved." Phew! Was I relieved! What's more, I liked our choice of name even better. Even though I only met the man once, I felt through our name a closeness and deeper connection to our Eternal Grand Master. It fit with the foundational concept I wanted our school to be built on. With my uncertainty resolved, the Seung-ri Black Belt Academy began operations and in 2004 we incorporated. It seems that nothing worth having ever comes easy. Somehow, there will always be a challenge attached to it, even if it's simply choosing a name. Along the way though, I had learned something more about the Korean language, and learning is always good.

My life's journey has taken me down many roads, some of them dead ends; one drove me to bankruptcy and some produced more than I ever could have hoped for. All were valuable learning experiences. In life as in business, we function and operate out of our core values. Whether we recognize, understand, or can articulate those values is another thing, but they are always operating consciously or unconsciously. I found over my time in taekwondo that there are two values that I've come to recognize in myself. They are "relentless" and "resilient." With all my internal doubts and fears and the times when I seem to lack confidence, when I'm at my lowest about to get swallowed up, somehow I've always found the strength, determination, and will to see the task through—most times successfully. This period of my life brought that understanding to me in clear relief.

"Don't mistake activity for accomplishment"

I had a greater sense of accomplishment in the past six years than I'd ever had in my twenty years playing music. That time had definitely been active as I'm not one for standing still, but I remember reading a quotation one day that said, "Don't mistake activity for accomplishment." That summed up my years in music. There had been high points and successes, but we were never able to sustain them or turn them into anything more than one-offs. Over the years on the road, I had been prepared to sacrifice many things in my drive to succeed. When things collapsed at the end, the thing I was not willing to sacrifice was my relationship with my wife and children, or my core values. Don't get me wrong, I did a lot of foolish, selfish things and made tons of mistakes over those years. Many of those things hurt those around me and I'm not proud of them, but I'll never deny that I did them. I thought success would make up for all those errors in judgment. I was wrong.

There was one fundamental thing that had been reignited in me over those past six years of training and study, a fundamental understanding that had a substantial and positive impact on my life. Studying and implementing the life skills concepts of courtesy, respect, integrity, perseverance, and (one I had never even considered as a life skill) goal setting all had a huge effect on my everyday life; one of these skills would become our focus for a testing cycle lasting eight weeks and for me they became life changing. Talking about them in class and working to incorporate them into our training affected my life in so many positive ways. Over the years, their impact has continued to increase, giving me the strength and resolve to overcome numerous challenges.

I now had firsthand experience and proof that writing down your goals can bring about the desired results. Here I was, a second degree black belt and business owner. Just as important as the titles was the re-establishment of other skills like respect, loyalty, and honor. I would need every one of them to make this undertaking more than wishful thinking. Every reward comes with a challenge. I still had to pay off Mr. Ford and more importantly I needed to learn how to attract more students. I thought it would be straightforward, but I soon learned that it's easier said than done.

For the next two years, I did PE classes and multicultural days in the local public schools. Gradually, the school grew from the original seven students to ten, and then up to twenty. Classes got so full that I had to add another night of training. We now trained Tuesday, Wednesday, and Thursday, and the club was full of students with strong, positive energy. I was becoming more comfortable with the position of club owner and gaining in confidence as an instructor. It's funny, we can have all manner of certifications and paper validations, but the way we feel inside about what we do and how we do it can be totally contrary to what we have hanging on our walls. It can be a bit of a paradox at times, but I was learning every day and slowly but surely paying Mr. Ford off. Soon I would own the club outright.

As the club grew and after I'd paid the rent, I put any extra money back into the school for updating equipment, purchasing mats, and other maintenance tasks. It would be years yet before I could draw a salary from the business. For now, the school was paying its bills and I was committed to delivering my papers as my way of contributing to the family's finances. Even though we could have used more income, I did not feel any reason to rush or push too hard. I had learned from my experience in the music business what pushing too hard can do. I had no intention of duplicating that experience.

Looking back, I feel going bankrupt was the best thing that ever happened to me. I'll admit that for the first three to four years afterwards I was a very bitter man. It took me a long time to work through my feelings of anger, frustration, embarrassment, and disappointment, but eventually I got there. For the greater portion of that time, I blamed everybody but myself, but gradually, as has been said many times before, "Time heals all wounds." I came to accept my responsibility for what had happened and owned it. That it was on my shoulders and no one else's was a large part of the healing process. It had always been my responsibility.

I've learned from working through those experiences that I had taken my success as a right. I thought it was my right to be successful, when in reality success was a privilege to be nurtured. I have come to understand that. Now that I have achieved a modicum of success, I am thankful everyday for what I have and work hard to continue to earn that success daily. As Carole and I worked our way through the bankruptcy, that fact became much clearer and I became more appreciative of the people and things I had around me, including what I was learning from my studies.

In December of 2002, I successfully tested for my third degree at the Gateway club. It was to be the last test for me at the club where

MASTERSHIP

I got my start. Mr. and Mrs. Ford would move to Edmonton in June of 2003. It had been almost seven years since I began training there. My son, Robert, had started his training in December of 1997 and had tested for his second degree black belt in August. Carole was now a first degree black belt, having started her training in March of 1999. We were a family that met two nights a week to train and improve our skills. It was a sad day when it all came to an end; when the last class was over, there were more than a few tears shed. The students of Gateway threw a going-away party, and then it was over. In those seven years, I had accomplished and grown more than at any time in my life up to then. It was a wonderfully gratifying time.

In 2002 and 2003, I got another chance to learn how to responsibly manage the incoming money. As I continued to learn fiscal responsibility, I was also learning how to deal with the hopes, dreams, and concerns of our parents and students, and how the fostering of constructive relationships helps build a business. In western culture, there is a misconception about taekwondo or any martial art for that matter. The arts are more about self-mastery than about being the biggest, meanest, toughest badass in the room. They teach us about when, where, and how to use our skill, whether that be mental, emotional, or physical. In our style, Mastership is about achieving the status of a Master Instructor not a master fighter. Of course, we also know how to defend ourselves and a great many of our senior ranks, myself included, have and do train in other styles like Krav Maga, Brazilian Jiu Jitsu, and Jeet Kune Do. Some have achieved significant levels of rank in those other disciplines. As long as the foundation in our schools is Songahm Taekwondo, we as school owners and instructors can pursue and train in other disciplines.

The years between 2002 and 2003 would allow me the time to think about the kind of curriculum I would like in a commercial school. What other martial art disciplines would work with Songahm. In a club that was operating three days a week for two to two and a half hours each day, it was enough to teach taekwondo. But in a commercial location, the space would be available for use seven days a week, twenty-four hours a day, allowing for greater flexibility in scheduling and curriculum. It would be a few years down the road before I would branch out into other styles. The first goal was to create a solid base of students to create the income to afford a commercial location. Making the move from a club to a full-on school increases the overhead costs considerably so, every chance I got, I squirreled away money, planning when I could make that commercial school happen.

In June of 2003, two events happened that would propel me into that commercial location sooner than I had ever anticipated. The first was being invited to one of our local schools to take part in their annual multicultural day, which I gladly accepted. I had done the same event the previous year, but this time the result would be quite different. It involved different cultural events in several classrooms for two hours in the morning (broken into two one-hour segments) and one hour in the afternoon, with students rotating between classrooms. In between, there would be a lunch break in which food from all the countries represented in the school would be available for the teachers, students, parents, and guest instructors to enjoy. The great thing was that all the food was prepared by the students and parents of the school. It was always a fun day and a great experience for everyone.

That day there must have been something magic in the air because it had never happened at any class I had done before, nor has it happened since. I did my regular presentation, beginning with giving the students a brief history lesson in the origins of taekwondo. Then I had them come to attention to demonstrate discipline and how the bow is done to show respect, which was the life skill that day. I then taught them a block for personal protection, combining it with a kick and a strike for their self-defense. When they demonstrated that knowledge, I had them practice on targets and then with partners, all the while reinforcing the life skill of respect. I taught all three classes that day and everyone in them seemed to have an enjoyable time. At the end of every class, I was allowed to hand out my business card, which offered them a free thirty-day trial.

Over the following couple of weeks, over twenty of those students took me up on my offer and came in for classes. Afterwards, they all wanted to enroll, but as it was the end of the school year, many would soon be off on summer vacations. They would not be able to train over the summer but wanted to register for our fall semester. In all, twenty new students gave me a $100 deposit to hold a place for them come September. That was the first large infusion of cash into the school. For me at that time, $2,000 was a large amount of money. The first thing I did was put it into the bank immediately. To add another boost to the bottom line a few weeks after the multicultural day, a parent came to me wanting to pay up front for the next ten months of training for herself and her son. She had just received a settlement and wanted to ensure they both had a spot.

From this parent, I learned just how valuable the training experience can be for some people. Between these two events happening within a short period, I was able to bank close to $4,000. I had never had that much money in a bank account that was not spoken for. You may find it a bit odd or even a little funny, but for me that was one of the most wonderful feelings I've ever had. I had a bank account with money in it—what a satisfying feeling!

That summer even though things slowed down as usual, with families taking vacations and spending time on the beach, I started to plan and dream about what it would be like to open a commercial school. Come September with the twenty new students, we would be close to thirty active members. I started to write down questions and concerns about what would be involved in opening a commercial school. Would the students I have now be enough to sustain moving the club into a commercial storefront space, allowing me to develop and grow? What would the costs be to open a location, buy mats, and get office furniture? What monthly expenses would be incurred in a commercial space? How many days would I be open—five or six days a week? How many classes per day? For me the most important question was how does one go about finding a location?

As summer moved into fall and the students returned, those thoughts were replaced with the everyday concerns of training, class plans, keeping the existing students motivated, and staying focused on growing the club. One night in early October, I was talking with one of the adult students about what I had written down over the summer.

Chris was a local businessman, and I had been speaking with him about a space for the past few months. Chris had many good relationships and contacts with some of the local realtors and was willing to do some research for me. He also had personal experience in locating space for his own restaurant business.

By the fall of 2003, we were beginning to outgrow the space I had been renting from a local church for two years. I had been unable to add any more days of training as the church was growing as well. Also we couldn't get the gym for our testing's as we had been accustomed to, so something had to give. We now had thirty active students. I had been running the club for over two years and it was growing as I had continued to develop my marketing and instruction skills over that time. By the fall of 2003, whether I liked it or not, I had to make a decision to have Chris actively start looking for a location that would meet the needs of what I took to be a growing martial arts school. I had so much more to learn.

Opening a school was something I definitely wanted to do, but I wondered if I had enough income from our existing students to sustain a commercial space. As much as I wanted to be, I knew I wasn't in a financial position to seriously consider looking into one. Even so, we continued to talk about it regularly over the next few weeks. I showed him the list of questions and concerns I had written down. Chris shared his personal experiences about locating a space and what's involved in the maintenance of a commercial business.

One night after class, Chris approached me and asked if I was okay with him beginning to look for a space on my behalf. He told me he had given a lot of thought to this and was prepared to invest $7,000 towards start-up costs. Of the $4,000 I had back in June, I now had $2,000 remaining, which brought us to a total of $9,000 for my working capital. With my limited business experience, I thought that was a lot of money, so Chris began to contact some local realtors and get the search underway. Looking back now over my fifteen years in business, I have come to realize just how little I knew and how truly fortunate I was. This was one time when ignorance was truly bliss, if I knew then what I know now, I would not have taken that step. I'm glad I didn't know.

MASTERSHIP

Mid-terming in Las Vegas, March 2000; executing a jump reverse side kick, and, yes, I broke the board

Black belt testing World Championship Little Rock, Arkansas, over four hundred black belts from around the world meet in Little Rock every June or July to challenge themselves mentally and physically

CHAPTER 5
A LEAP OF FAITH

"Energy and persistence conquer all things."

—*Benjamin Franklin*

On March 1, 2004, at the age of fifty-seven, I took a complete leap of faith and opened my first business. It was located at 1430 Johnston Road in White Rock, BC. As with all leaps of faith, you can count on it being tested somewhere along the line. Mine would be greatly tested within the first six months of opening the doors. Running a club out of a church is, as I would quickly find out, a nice hobby; running a commercial business would be a whole different animal. The opening of our new location had been greatly facilitated by Chris, not only from a financial perspective, but also by his belief in what I would later come to understand was my vision. He had started his training under Mr. Ford and was one of the original seven students who were there when I purchased the White Rock club. Chris not only saw my vision but had experienced what the training can give and bring to an individual. To this day, he is my most loyal and trusted friend and business advisor, his two young daughters are now training with us.

The process took some time but by late November of 2003 Chris had found what we thought was a suitable space and negotiations were started. I had as much experience in negotiating a lease as I did in business (none), so I was fortunate and thankful to have Chris there to help guide me through it all. The space was 2,400 square feet located behind a pet store. It had been vacant for a number of years and, with the removal of one non-load-bearing wall and a fresh coat of paint, we felt it could be made suitable for our needs. By early January of 2004, an agreement was reached on a five-year lease that would see me take possession on February 1, 2004. We would have a month to do the needed work to prepare the unit for classes and I would have three months free rent. Over those three months, we would however be paying the monthly common costs. My goal and hope was that over the three months of March, April, and May, I could enroll more students and get the new location off to a strong start. I would be doing a show-and-tell at an elementary school about a block from our new location a week before I was to open, so things looked promising; I was very hopeful.

When you sign a commercial lease, standard procedure is to pay the first and last months' rent up front, so the first cheque was approximately $4,800, which took a huge bite out of the available $9,000 seed money. That left me $4,200 to do leasehold improvements and purchase the training floor. I remember telling Carole when I was writing out the lease cheques for the coming year's payments, "I guess this is going to work, because my arm hasn't fallen off as I wrote them." I had never in my life written a year's worth of cheques that totaled close to $29,000.

Today with my son, we presently own two martial arts academies that are both run purposely with small overdraft limits of under $10,000. We will go into the red sometimes, but at the end of every month, we are in the black. We have two academy credit cards, one US and one Canadian; no matter what the balance, they are paid off every month on their due dates. I personally have a small line of credit and one credit card, which I do my best to pay off every month. It doesn't always happen, but I most certainly don't run it up. The lesson learned from the bankruptcy was to pay your bills on time and don't spend what you don't have. At that time though I only had a personal credit card

MASTERSHIP

with a very small credit line and I would soon have cause to question my sanity and this decision.

The month of February was spent doing the needed renovations. We were fortunate as we only had to remove one wall and wash everything down (it had been vacant for many years). We could then put a fresh coat of paint on all the walls and lastly lay down the training floor. With the help of Chris, Carole, and a number of the students and parents, we were able to accomplish all the tasks in time. I opened the doors to my business on March 1, 2004, with very high hopes. There had been a lot of hard work to get the space ready. The $9,000 was gone. I had no cash reserves and no line of credit yet, and somehow I thought the hard work was over. What a rookie. I was about to learn that what we had done was just a warm up and nothing compared to what I was about to face. The heavy lifting was just about to begin.

I spoke at the end of the last chapter about how I've learned over the years just how fortunate I was to start a business the way I did. In truth it was a recipe for disaster and failure, but with a miracle I pulled it off. Throughout my years in business, when I have spoken to other school owners in our organization or other business owners in general, I have been flat-out told I was stone-cold crazy. They have no idea how I was able to pull it off and succeed. At the time, I didn't know any better, and with my passion and ignorance I just went for it. I guess what I didn't know didn't hurt me. As I said earlier, if I'd known then the amount of work, stress, and sleepless nights I'd experience from committing to do this, even with all my passion and enthusiasm, I highly doubt I would have ever started the journey. I didn't know, though, and so I took the leap and got started. Along the way, there would be one defining moment that would take place that, to this day, I simply can't explain. In that moment, it was of immense help, giving me the impetus I needed to succeed. More on that in a bit.

I love the arts, and more importantly I love Songahm Taekwondo and Eternal Grand Master's vision of "Creating tomorrow's leaders one black belt at a time." In developing Songahm Taekwondo, he created a second chance at life for me. I'm sure that he created something just as unique for every one of the students of Songahm, whether they stayed students or became instructors or school owners.

I started the Seung-ri Academy not because I was a good businessman, but because Songahm Taekwondo had helped me through one of the most difficult periods of my life. It literally turned my life around and sent me off in an entirely different direction. It re-invigorated my life and gave me back my self esteem and a positive focus. Somehow, I had to give back. Somehow, I needed to find a way to create the opportunity for others to experience it for themselves. Little did I know that the education I was about to receive and the test I was about to be put through would create that experience for others. I'd taken my leap of faith and now the real test was about to begin.

Every morning from opening day, I would arrive at the academy at 9 AM to open the doors. I would sit and study some of the marketing materials that came from HQ. I would work on what I thought would be the best ad for our local newspaper, one that would represent the idea of my business. I would figure out the biggest size I could afford and then decide how long I could afford to run it. That was the extent of my marketing knowledge other than doing show-and-tells. For my first few months in business, I ran ads in the local newspaper. Needless to say, they didn't produce one phone call. Live and learn. I'd question the ads: their size and shape and the content. Was it the placement or was it the demographic? So much to learn, so much to understand, so much I didn't know, so little time to make it happen—but I had to keep working at it. Sometimes it's not what you do but more what you're willing to do that pays off in the end. I just kept striving to make that connection any way I could with our community. Later I came to understand that the demographic I needed to reach didn't read the newspaper. Nonetheless, I was there every day, five days a week, doing whatever I could think of but not really having any concept or concrete plan or idea of what needed to be done. Some days I would do some personal training and then work on designing the curriculum and class plans—anything to keep me motivated, active, and feeling as if I was doing something constructive. I was confusing activity with accomplishment.

MASTERSHIP

A few months of being there every day and not producing any results began to take its toll on me. I was spending money advertising in the local paper. I was doing show-and-tells and PE classes. I was doing everything and anything that I could think of to raise my hand and say, "Take a look at this!" My efforts were not enough to bring about the positive results I had planned for over those first few months. Gradually, I began to lose the confidence and enthusiasm I'd had; this was not the way I had envisioned it all developing. In reality though I had never truly envisioned much more than having a place where people could come, workout, train, and learn.

Knowing little to nothing of marketing, networking, or business in general, I was truly up against it. I loved Songahm Taekwondo and had a desire to share that love and passion with others, but I didn't know how. Originally, that's what drove me to show up every morning. Now, I was showing up because I had to. I'd sit and watch the world walk by the window, wondering what I was doing wrong. What was I missing? What could I do? How could I draw some attention to the academy and make something happen?

Mr. Ford would phone from Edmonton every now and again with words of encouragement, but I was the one on the ground who had to figure it out. I was struggling. In fact, I was becoming depressed. Why wouldn't anyone walk through the door? Why didn't the ads work? Why weren't the show-and-tells producing any interest?

The odd time someone would come in, but it was generally a mistake and they would be looking for Randy, the dog groomer next door. For four months (March, April, May, and June), I don't recall enrolling one new student. When I put my plan together back in 2003, I had optimistically projected I would have enrolled between twenty to thirty new students by this point. This would have given me between fifty to sixty students actively training within the first four months of opening. I'd naïvely thought people who were interested in martial arts would find me and give me a chance to show them what the academy was all about and the benefits of the training. As of May 2004, I had fewer than thirty students and summer was fast approaching, when many students generally take a break—meaning they would want to stop paying. As of June 1, I would be paying the full rent of $2,400 per month. I had enough saved up from not having to pay full rent for March, April, and May to cover June and July, and if I managed the July income properly, I should make Augusts' payment.

At that time in my business development, I knew little about agreements or contracts. So when parents came to me to say they would be taking the summer off, they expected me to stop their payments—and I did. I was that green that I simply capitulated, which would leave me cash poor. After just making the August 1 rent, I knew from the available income from the students who were still training that I was not going to make the September payment. Six months into my first commercial venture and I was in the process of failing. I was worn out, heart sick, and terrified. Here was my test of faith that came from taking the leap. I was beginning to lose my faith in what I set out to do and in my ability to do it. I was scared just thinking about it as once again I was looking straight into the face of another failure. Once again, I knew the sick feeling of fear. Every day I faithfully went to the academy and every day I struggled to think of what I could I do to change this picture. Every day I wondered how to get new students. Many times that summer I taught classes to just one student. Five classes, five students. Every day I fought not let this happen, but I didn't have an answer.

By the middle of the month, there was no improvement and there didn't seem to be any hope on the horizon. If I had any faith left, I had trouble finding it. I didn't talk to or tell anyone. How do you tell someone that you're failing again? There didn't seem to be an answer coming or a quick fix available, other than an infusion of cash. Even knowing that, I was not about to approach anyone to borrow money for what appeared to be a ship dead in the water. If there was a quick infusion of cash, it would not correct the root problem, which was the ability to get new students in the door. I was at a total loss.

I had now been open for half a year and over that time I hadn't even had enough available cash to purchase an outside mailbox so the mailman could drop off my mail if I wasn't there. Sometimes the mailman would leave it with Randy the dog groomer next door if I wasn't there. I had come to know Randy and he was a good guy. He graciously offered to collect my mail for me and I could swing by and pick it up, or he'd slip it through the circulation vent windows over my front door. It was a workable relationship.

On a mid-August morning right around my birthday, I walked into the academy with a heavy heart. I was two weeks away from having to tell my landlord that I didn't have the rent. I was starting to count the days as if they were nails in my coffin. I had even started planning what I was going to say. I was isolated, alone, and scared. That morning as I turned on the lights, I noticed an envelope on the floor with the word September written on it in big bold letters. It had obviously been flipped through the open vents. As I bent down to pick it up, I noticed it was thick and soft. My curiosity grew as I opened it. I almost fell over when I saw what was inside. I stood there in stunned disbelief, trying to catch my breath. It was full of cash, and a fair amount by the looks of it. Inside there were fifty-five $20 bills, along with one $10 bill and a loonie (a Canadian $1 coin) for a total of $1,111. It's a moment in my life I will never forget. I just stood there in shock. Where had this money come from? Would someone walk through the door in a minute asking for it back? I don't know how long I stood there looking at what I held in my hand, waiting for someone to walk through the door and reclaim it, but no one did.

No one knew the situation I was facing as I hadn't spoken to anyone about it, not even Carole. How could I? I couldn't burden her with another pending failure and I hadn't spoken to anyone simply because there was no one I trusted enough. I didn't want to admit the fact that all my hopes and dreams were dissolving in front of me. I thought I was the only one who knew how desperate things were. Yet somehow, here was over $1,000 cash dropped in my lap. To this day, I still don't where it came from. Over those months of doing a lot praying and much soul-searching, God was the only one I had shared my doubts and fears with.

Maybe it was my pride or maybe I was too embarrassed to admit that once again it appeared I'd overstepped my abilities. Had I taken things too lightly? I don't know what stopped me from opening up to someone, but I hadn't. How long I stood there waiting to wake up from what seemed like a dream, I can't tell you. Eventually, I pulled myself back together and sat down. I finally accepted that what I was holding in my hand was real and there was no one standing beside me asking for it back. I could think of only one thing to do, which was to go straight to the bank and deposit it. That's exactly what I did.

The kicker came when I deposited the money into the school's account. It was to the dollar exactly what was needed to cover September's rent. Somehow, in some manner, my faith, training and discipline had seen me through. I hadn't quit or given up. I had remained dedicated to my vision. If there was one student in class, he got the best I could give as I worked through my doubts and fears. Somehow it seemed I had passed a test; my trust and faith had been tested to its maximum, but it had also been rewarded. To this day, I have no explanation. Right then at the teller's wicket, something told me I was going to make it. I was going to be all right. For me it was God saying that He had my back. I knew then I had to figure out this business thing now.

Filled with new energy and confidence, I went back to the school and framed that envelope. I hung it on the office wall as a reminder to myself of the day when all hope seemed lost. It still hangs on my office wall to this day. When things get tough, I look at that envelop and remember that gift, that miracle, that honor and know, if I stay true to my vision and put my best effort in, it will be all right.

As soon as it was hung, I got to work. I went online and started to research business courses. It was time to learn, it was time to grow, and it was time to get down to business in a serious way.

MASTERSHIP

Framed September envelope the contained the $1111

Robert with some of our leadership team at a local community event, raising our businesses profile; this was one of the ways we got down to business

CHAPTER 6
GOING COMMERCIAL—THE BIRTH OF THE BUSINESS

"Faith in the end game helps you live through the months or years of the buildup."

—Jim Collins

Since that August day in 2004, I have spent tens of thousands of dollars on business courses, seminars, and coaches. I have become a voracious reader, reading anything about business or personal development that I can lay my hands on that will improve my business or personal knowledge, inspire me, or give me some new insight. Over the past twelve years, I have amassed a library of books on business, leadership, and self-improvement. You've heard it said that necessity is the mother of invention; well, in the fall of 2004, I started to re-invent myself as a businessman. I became proactive through continual reading and study. Even though I couldn't afford them at that time, I would look for business courses online or coaches/mentors—anything that would help plan my future and give me a perspective to the underlying foundation of a successful business and deepen my knowledge on growing in business. One day I knew I would be able to and I wanted to make an informed choice.

In the martial arts world, September can always be counted on to bring an influx of new students. Parents start looking for after-school activities for their children. The September of 2004 was no different, and once the school year started I experienced a slow but steady growth over the following three months. That, along with the students who returned from their summer holidays, brought the school's finances back into the black, which lessened my stress level considerably. Classes were filling and that helped push good energy through the school.

In opening the school, my primary objective was and continues to be to create a place where people can experience the benefits of Songahm Taekwondo. I wanted to create an environment where students of all ages would feel comfortable yet challenged, a space where families could train and grow stronger together. It has never been about the money. Now obviously I'm not stupid (naïve, maybe) and I learned rather quickly just how important money is to a business. By going through the summer of 2004, I learned that lesson well. In all honesty though, money was never my driving force and that remains true to this day.

However, I knew I had to become knowledgeable about running a successful business. I started by reading, which at that time was the most economical way to begin my education and watch the expenses. The more I read, the more I gained. I was also gaining daily in experience. Every day that I could open the doors and teach class was a blessing, but the process was slow. I needed someone to talk to, to hold me accountable and support me. Where would I find someone like that? I could look at the local colleges for courses, but I taught at night, so night school was not an option, and during the day I needed to focus on my business. Where and how could I begin my research?

By the fall of 2004, I had just turned fifty-seven, a time when most people look forward to retiring. Instead, I was looking forward to learning how to make my business work. It became my driving force as I certainly didn't want to deliver papers for the remaining years of my life. At my age, no one was going to hire or train me for anything more than a minimum wage job.

MASTERSHIP

I have a passion for people's well-being as well as taekwondo, and I was gaining experience in overcoming mental and emotional obstacles. That was something I was determined to share. I had passed through my test of faith and faced down the doubts, fears, and challenges. Words cannot adequately express what I experienced in finding that envelop on the floor in August 2004. It would be many years before I would share that experience with others. It was still so hard to believe. The confidence, reassurance, and renewed faith that came from that moment in time helped to propel me forward. My vision was still intact; now if I could learn how to make my business grow, then teaching and running the business would be something I could do for the rest of my life.

By the spring of 2005, I had read a few books on business. One that struck a chord with me was *The E-Myth* by Michael Gerber. Although in theory it made sense to me (the concept of "working on your business not in your business"), I really didn't understand how to go about implementing what he recommended. Knowledge is one thing, but experience is totally different and, for the most part, it was beyond my scope of experience. One thing that became clear to me from reading the book was that I wanted and needed more help than could be found through reading. I needed a real person to talk to, a coach. To that end, I started where everyone starts—by getting back online. I had started to research different online business courses in the fall of 2004, but I couldn't afford them then. Now I was in a better financial position, so I once again used Google to do some research and began making notes.

Within a couple of days of research, I settled on a course through the E-Myth Corporation called "Embark." I contacted them and found that the course ran for six months and cost $1,500 USD. I would work with a dedicated coach one-on-one for thirty minutes once a week over the phone. Of all the courses I had looked at, this one contained what I thought were the foundational pillars of a successful business. The course material covered leadership, money, management, marketing, client fulfillment, lead generation, and lead conversion. I hoped it would help me put a stronger foundation under my business. It was a good place to start. I could download and print all the study materials, and there would be online tests to give me immediate and direct feedback. The best thing was having a coach, someone to not only hold me accountable but also explain things when I had trouble grasping the concepts. The course material covered all the areas that were important to me and a successful completion would be the cornerstone to my business. For me, it was Business 101 and, as I hadn't found anything even close to what the course offered, I signed up and got to work in the spring of 2005.

This was the first of many courses and programs I would invest time and money in over the coming years. Every time I always asked myself, "Is this the best use of the available money? Is this what I need to learn? Am I smart enough to learn this?" The answer that always came back to me was, "You can't afford not to." Sometimes I risked my balance sheet because of the price of a course or a coach, but I have never regretted any of the money I spent. I have always received some gem of knowledge that has helped me grow as a person or helped me improve my business.

Throughout the spring and summer of 2005, my knowledge and confidence about business began to grow as did the business itself. I began to feel like I could run a successful business and things were firming up under my feet. The student body was growing and there were now forty active students training. I had put a credit policy in place for those families who wished to take the summer off that would ensure a steady cash flow throughout the summer while at the same time giving them credit for monies paid. It was a win-win situation. It had been a challenging yet rewarding couple of years, but the hard work and money invested in the future of the business had begun to pay dividends. That along with the growing student body filled me with hope for tomorrow. Growth, stability, and consistency—if I could establish these three things, I would do just fine.

MASTERSHIP

Robyn, Carole, me, and Robert at the conclusion of my fourth degree black belt ceremony at the White Rock school

Many old students from the Gateway club came together at my fourth degree ceremony to see Mr. Ford (right hand side in uniform)

CHAPTER 7
GROWTH AND STABILITY

"Strength and growth come only through continuous effort and struggle."

—*Napoleon Hill*

The success that the school experienced through 2005 was attributable to an improved ability to market. We brought in more students, which gave me the ability to focus on serving them more effectively. That in turn brought in more students through word of mouth, which is the best kind of marketing. This increased success generated enough cash flow that we had the money to do some leasehold improvements. The first thing I wanted to do was create more space by expanding the training floor area.

It's a great thing for any business to grow, but that can be quickly negated by a poor service experience. After the initial challenges of opening the 1430 Johnston location, the school had grown steadily throughout the fall and winter of 2004 and into 2005, so much so that by the summer of 2006 something had to give. We needed to remove some old office walls to make more training floor space available. When we took possession of the 1430 Johnston space, I got the impression that the last tenant was a business that had used some kind of photographic chemicals. There was a back room that could easily have been a dark room. It had tap connection outlets and a drain pipe to attach a sink to, and chemical stains covered the floor. In the front, there were three small offices upon entering. In removing those office walls, we would be adding another 800 square feet to the training area. This would give our existing students more space to train in and allow more students on the floor at the same time.

In the first week of August in 2006, we closed for a week to facilitate these renovations. One of my oldest students, Pat, had offered to help. He was a subcontractor and understood the necessary steps for removing the walls properly and the correct procedure for re-routing the electrical wires. It took the entire week to finish it, but we got it done and were ready to open again by the next week, new training floor and all.

> **"It's the people we surround ourselves with that help to facilitate our success or failure"**

Without the people around me like Chris and Pat (who is now operating his own club and is still a student with me) and our parent group over the years, there wouldn't be a story to tell. It's the people we surround ourselves with that help to facilitate our success or failure. I have been fortunate over these past twenty years to have had some fine people buy into and believe in the benefits of the wonderful art of Songahm Taekwondo. I did not make this happen alone; all of us made it happen.

One of the key people without whom I could never have accomplished any of this is my son, Robert. He started his training in Songahm Taekwondo when he was eight. He was being bullied at school, and Carole and I thought that doing martial arts might give him the confidence to stand strong, which it did. I remember three instances that demonstrated not only his ability to stand up for himself but also how to be responsible.

The first came one summer day in 1999 when he was ten and coming home from a day at the local outdoor pool. He told me he had struck a boy on his arm with a hammerfist, hitting his radial nerve, as the boy was trying to dunk him for a second or third time after Robert had told him to stop. He then told me he immediately found the lifeguard and said, "My name is Robert Davidson and I hit that boy on his radial nerve because was trying to dunk me after I'd told him to stop. I thought you should know."

A second situation arose when he was in high school and he was running across the school grounds. The way he related it to me was that two boys decided they didn't like the way he was running and decided to take issue with him. One was on a bike and one was running, and both were coming at him from different angles. Robert realized that the boy who was running was going to get to him first. He assessed the situation and positioned himself to address the boy who was running. When he got there, Robert gave him a round kick to the midsection, doubling him over and stopping the other boy in his tracks. Once the boys realized they'd chosen the wrong person to pick on, Robert went straight to the office. Much like the swimming pool incident, he told the staff who he was and what had happened. The school brought the three boys together and got things straightened out shortly after. In both situations, I was extremely proud not only of his ability to stand up and protect himself but that he took responsibility for his actions.

The third was when at fifteen after training consistently for seven years, he attained his second degree black belt in 2002. He told me he was going to take a break from his training to focus on school. He wanted to apply the mental skills he'd learned from his training to improve his schoolwork. He decided to set a goal of getting on the honor roll. His mom and I gave him our blessing. School had never come easily for him so we both gave him our full support. For the next two years, he dedicated himself solely to the accomplishment of that goal, and when he graduated in 2004, it was with honors. His mom and I were both very proud, not only that he'd graduated with honors, but that he had the discipline to set a goal and accomplish it. These were skills he'd learned over his seven years of taekwondo training, and he had obviously learned them well.

Upon graduating, his plan was to attend university back in New York State to be close to a young lady he had met. He had an interest in psychology and wanted to pursue a career in that field. I remember telling him at the time, if he was really interested in learning psychology, to get in front of a class and teach. I told him he would learn a lot about people from that position and be able to positively affect people's lives. He obviously gave it some thought because, a little while later, he informed me he'd like to help at the school for a year and spend that time working towards his black collar certified instructor status before going to the states.

That year turned into three as he and the young lady had parted ways. In May of 2007, he achieved his goal of certified instructor black collar. He was awarded his new uniform on July 13, 2007. It was a proud day for our family. Over those three years, he had become a valuable part of the school, assisting in many of the classes and teaching the others, which gave me the opportunity to set enrollment or upgrade appointments. As well, his computer skills were far superior to mine and was helpful in organizing our databases, as was his creation of our marketing materials.

Over those years, I watched him grow into a fine young man and instructor whose training had brought him to a place where he could develop a career if he so choose, but that would be up to him. In his ten years of training he had learned many valuable life skills, such as perseverance, integrity, and self-control. Skills that he could take anywhere he wanted to go and be successful.

In 2005, Carole and I had the good fortune to buy our first home in White Rock, a small condo that was a two-minute walk from the school and would comfortably accommodate Robert, Carole, and me. We had been able to accomplish this through the income generated from Carole's job and the help of family with the down payment. Kat and Robyn had sprouted their wings a few years back and were out making their way in the world. Kat had married a few years earlier but had recently separated and was raising her young three-year-old daughter, Aria, while working for a local school board and attending university in the evenings. Robyn had moved in with her future husband and was attending a local university, working towards her accounting degree.

By 2006, the school was generating enough revenue that I was able quit the papers and pay myself from the company. This allowed me to dedicate all my time and effort to improving my business skills and focus solely on the school. For the next while, I paid myself exactly what I received from delivering papers—a little under $1,000 per month. As Robert was still living at home, we agreed that until the school met a certain income benchmark, he would not draw any money from the business. Instead, we invested what extra money we had to work on improving our business skills through various courses and coaches. I continued building my reading library, never being satisfied with the knowledge I had or thinking that I knew enough. If we were going to earn a good living and be able to maintain and grow a business, then I felt we should always be learning. Colin Powell stated it very well when he said, "There are no secrets to success. It's the result of preparation, hard work, and learning from failure."

By 2007, the school had grown to seventy active students. We were generating enough consistent income that I was able to start paying my son a wage and give myself a small increase as well. There was a confidence building between Robert and me that we could take our work ethic and our love for taekwondo and develop it into a sustainable business. Ever so gradually, this was becoming a reality.

> **"There are no secrets to success. It's the result of preparation, hard work, and learning from failure."**
> **—Colin Powell**

In February of 2007, I would pass my fourth degree test at Spring Nationals in Las Vegas. As much as I trained to be better in business, I would continually challenge myself to continue my progression through the ranks. I felt that growth and development in both aspects of my new life were intertwined; they needed to progress together. One of the ways I kept motivated to test was to attend our region's tournaments. Our region contained three states and one province: Idaho, Oregon, Washington, and BC. I competed in forms, weapons, and sparring at these tournaments, which kept me engaged in our region but also performing and setting an example that it had nothing to do with age and everything to do with attitude. In 2007, I would turn sixty.

As 2007 moved into 2008, our business along with our wages continued to grow. We were now coming into our fourth year of being in business. Gone were the days of worry and concern for our cash flow.

Over the years, I had been able to arrange a small line of credit with my bank so we now had a cushion to protect us during the times in a month when cash was in short supply. I tried once to have the line of credit increased, but I thought better of it and have left it where it was ever since. Our goal is to make the money we earn work for us, not go into debt. Every so often, we would dip into our line of credit, but by the end of the month we would make sure we were back in the black. If bankruptcy taught me nothing else, it was to pay the bills off every month and not use credit to pay them.

In the late summer of 2008, I was approached by another friend and martial arts school owner named Jason. He asked me if I would be interested in opening another location in the area. The space he was referring to was presently occupied by another style of martial arts. The owner of the building, Sam, just happened to be a business coach of mine from the past year. Apparently, he was having issues with the present tenant and would not be renewing their lease.

At first, I wasn't sure. I was worried because it was only a five-minute drive from our White Rock school. There were questions I needed to have answered. The most obvious one was how long I had to reply one way or the other. I quickly learned that there was no rush as the present tenant's lease wouldn't come up for renewal until February of 2009. I had plenty of time to think it over, so I let it be known that I was interested and I'd get back to him within the next couple of months with a decision.

It did interest me as I liked the idea of having two schools within close proximity, like Starbucks. The second question was; were we drawing any of our present students from this area? We were able to see the answer quickly using a simple exercise one of our coaches had us do a couple of years back. He'd recommended we get a map of our community and put colored pins in it to identify and track where all our students were coming from. Immediately, we were able to see that none of our existing student base came from that part of the community. That was definitely a positive sign. We also knew that there were three other martial arts schools in the area. That was not counting the one whose space we would be taking over. They were all within a one-block radius of each other. The competition would be greater than in White Rock, where we only had one other school to compete against. That being said, the existing school had a student body of approximately one hundred and fifty students—almost fifty percent more than the White Rock School—so I knew it was a viable location. It was definitely worth serious consideration and was enticing to think about.

On the downside, I would be unavailable to teach at White Rock, which meant Robert wouldn't have anyone to back him up. The White Rock School had finally reached a point of stability over this last year. We had seen consistent, steady growth; our students and parents were happy; and our bank account was stable. We had turned a profit the last couple of years and things were looking good. If we decided to take this step, there would be major adjustments. Our overhead would increase considerably; the rent alone was $2,000 a month higher than the White Rock School. Yes, there would be greater visibility and far more parking, but all that meant nothing without students to pay for it. All our bills would be duplicated—two rents, phones, hydro, internet, and insurance. There was a great deal to consider, both from the pro and con sides. Robert and I spent a lot of time talking about it. I spent considerable time in prayer as I firmly believed that this was something I could not decide to do without some serious prayer and meditation. If we decided to proceed, we would once again be taking a big risk, not to mention the threat it was to what we already had. I needed to believe that we could do it and were up to the challenge.

I quickly learned that, when you move from the position of a club to a full-on commercial enterprise, there is more that needs to be done in preparation. As I had found out with the White Rock School, nothing is as easy as it looks. If we were to go forward with opening a second location, I didn't want to leave anything to chance. I would need to draw on the experiences and knowledge I had gained from the first venture. In thinking seriously about this step, my first priority would be to make sure I used what I knew to think through all the pros and cons of what starting up a new venture could entail. Secondly, I would want to have considerably more financial resources available than I did when I first opened in White Rock. By now we had a savings account with available cash if needed and, over the years, we had developed a good business relationship with our bank; so I was pretty confident that if we were to proceed, there would be funds available.

In 2008, our regional organization had five commercial schools and multiple clubs throughout the Greater Vancouver region. One of the local club owners, who had a thriving club, heard that I was considering opening a second location and wanted to meet with me. He approached me about partnering if and when I decided to go forward. He had hopes one day of opening his own commercial school and thought this might be a good introduction to that world. I had known this instructor for many years so I said I would let him know when I had made my decision whether or not I was going to proceed with the new location. I would turn sixty-one in August and having a partner might help to take some of the workload off my shoulders. There was a lot to think about.

I had learned a lot over these past four years about my own capabilities and about the business world. I had watched my son grow into a fine, capable young man with a future in the martial arts if that's what he wanted to pursue. The most important thing though was realizing that success does not necessarily always have to be a young man's game, that it's more about attitude, energy, and resilience than youth. At sixty-one, I felt I was just getting my feet underneath me and there was much more that I could do.

After a training session with two of our senior ranks from HQs—on the left, Senior Master Abair and, on the right, Chief Master Droege

Mrs. Bennett, MP, Russ Hiebert, and me after a testing at the White Rock school

CHAPTER 8
WORLD CHAMPION

"Today not possible, tomorrow possible."
—*Eternal Grand Master H.U. Lee*

In the spring of 2005, I attended Spring Nationals for a second time as a tournament competitor. I had attended Spring Nationals back in 2000 to do a mid-term and compete; in 2000 I had come home with a couple of cracked ribs from some well placed side kicks. This tournament would bring a much different result and start me on a personal journey that would cover the next six years. Until that time, I had only competed at regional tournaments throughout BC, Washington, and Oregon, and I had always placed in the top three. That being said, there weren't probably more than three to five competitors in that age bracket (50–59) in our region to begin with, so placing in the top three did not present much of a challenge.

When a student is enrolled in the leadership program, they can accumulate points for every sanctioned tournament in which they place first, second, or third. Points are awarded in descending order. For a Class B regional tournament, 5 points for first, 3 points for second, and 1 point for third. Spring Nationals was a sanctioned AA tournament, so points awarded for first, second, and third are higher than the regional Class B.

I still considered myself a rookie, having only competed one other time on a national level, so I didn't have any great expectations. That day we had a ring of fifteen competitors from all over the United States—Texas, Florida, California, Michigan, etc.—I was the only Canadian and didn't know a soul.

Here's a little background on how the rings were run in 2005. The competitors could compete in three disciplines: forms, weapons, and sparring. The forms competition is always first, followed by weapons, and then sparring. In forms, the competitors each perform their form one at a time. To give the judges a gauge as to the caliber of the ring, the first three competitors will demonstrate their form before being scored. Once the first three have finished their forms, they are then brought up as a group and given their individual scores, setting a benchmark for those who follow. After that each competitor will be judged at the completion of their form. There are three judges to a ring: Judge A judges kicks and stances, Judge B judges blocks and strikes, and the Center Judge judges the overall performance and attitude of the competitor.

That day I was the first competitor up. I did my form and waited for the next two to complete their form; then the three of us were called up and given our scores. After that, I sat down, never giving my score a second thought, my thinking being there were twelve more competitors left and I wouldn't be there at the end so I'd just enjoy the experience. As the forms competition was getting closer to the last few competitors, a couple of the other more experienced competitors came over to me a told me that I was tied for first place.

"What!" No way. The first guy up is seldom around at the end and seldom gets scores that would put him in the running for third, let alone first, but as it turned out, they were correct. To be truthful, once I had finished, I hadn't even paid attention to my scores nor was I paying attention to anyone else's for that matter. Like I said, I was fifty-eight years old and still a rookie. That would be the last time I didn't keep my head in the game when competing. At the completion of the forms competition, sure enough, I was tied for first place with Mr. Robustelli from Florida, so we both had to do our forms again and the judges

MASTERSHIP

would then point to the winner. It was hard for me to comprehend, but there I was tied for first at a national event, go figure. I was first to go up and then Mr Robustelli. My form was strong and precise. After watching Mr. Robustelli, I felt I had a chance, now it was in the hands of the judges. At the completion of both forms, Mr. Robustelli and I were called up. The judges all stood and would point to the first place winner. Hard as it was for me to believe, two out of the three pointed to me. I'd won! I couldn't believe it. It was surreal; I was stunned. This was something I had never pictured in my wildest dreams. I'd won first place at a national event. I was walking on air for the rest of the day and went home with a first place trophy.

Our tournament year runs a full year from World Championship (June–July) to World Championship (June–July of the following year). As mentioned earlier, every time a competitor who is in the leadership program places either first, second, or third they are awarded points. If over the tournament year a competitor accumulates enough points, they can end up in the top ten of their division. Until that tournament, I was not in the top ten of mine, but after my first place finish, I was. The ten points I received from placing first propelled me into the top ten of my division (50–59). I would continue to compete and place in every tournament until the end of April in the 2005 tournament year. By doing so, I would remain in the top ten for the balance of the 2004/05 tournament year. Achieving top ten status would allow me to attend World Championships and compete for the title of World Champion in my division. I couldn't wait. Until Spring Nationals, I had never thought about top ten. I had known about it but never paid much attention to it; I just enjoyed competing. But now I was and wanted to be World Champ in a big way. I immediately began preparing by starting to look over my division online. There were names I recognized from Spring Nationals and some I didn't; nonetheless, I began to train and visualize success for the upcoming competition.

Attending Worlds that year was special for me; nine years into my second life and I was going to compete for World Champion. What a thrill. The top ten competition is held on the Friday before the new tournament season begins on Saturday. All the competitors go to their assigned rings to be checked in; once confirmed, the competition can begin. That year, if I remember correctly, I was in seventh place, which meant I would be fourth up as the competitors perform in descending order (10, 9, 8, 7 etc.). This format gives the number one ranked competitor the opportunity to know what he has to beat to take the title.

That year it wouldn't be me. I competed well but came in second—so close, but definitely not the result I came for. Naturally, it was disappointing; the goal was World Champ. But my finish was an improvement of five places, and I held my head high. The experience just wetted my appetite. I was going to be World Champ no matter what it took nor how long. I started by competing the following Sunday in forms, weapons, and sparring, as there is a top ten division in all disciplines. Worlds is a AAA sanctioned tournament, so taking first place is fifteen points, second is ten, and third is five. I cannot remember the placings that day, but I know I placed in the top three in forms and weapons, which was a great way, point wise, to start off the tournament year.

I came home with a Silver Medal and placement in the top three in forms and weapons to start the new tournament year. Upon returning home, I marked off all the upcoming tournaments and began to prepare myself for the local tournament season. To me, victories are only as good as what you accomplish after achieving them and I was not one to rest on my laurels.

For the next five years, I would attend World Championships, sometimes starting in tenth place, sometimes in first place, but my World Champion title would continue to elude me. The year I started in tenth place, I held first place until the very last competitor who held the first place ranking; he would beat me by one point. Aaargh. All the disappointments just seemed to motivate me even more. I would come home more determined than ever to accomplish that goal. I would not be denied.

In 2010, I again attended the World Championship. I was in the middle of the pack. When I did my form, the judges' scores vaulted me into first place. I was still there at the end of the competition, but I was in a tie for first place with a man from Texas. This meant we both had to go again. Just like at Spring Nationals in 2005, I was the first

MASTERSHIP

to go and my fellow competitor went second. My form felt good, but the competitor from Texas had a strong form as well; still I felt I had a chance. We stood side by side, waiting for the judges' decision. The judges stood to point to who would become the new World Champion. I held my breath. The Center Judge called for the score and two out of three pointed to me! I had done it! I had climbed that mountain and was standing on top of it. Finally, I was a World Champ, six years in the making. I was ecstatic! What a tremendous feeling of accomplishment and elation. Six years of challenging and preparing myself, day in and day out, year in and year out, of overcoming the disappointments and coming back stronger, of coming close, so close to almost touching it but not finishing. That now was all in the past. This time I had done it. YAHOO!

For the moment, my celebration had to be short-lived as, in a couple of `hours; I would be competing in top ten for weapons and sparring as well. Finding a quiet place where I could relax, collect my thoughts, and recover was a challenge. I needed to start preparing myself for the next two competitions. I found a place that was removed from the noise and closed my eyes, took some very deep breaths, and visualized my next rounds. The previous year I had tied for first in weapons but in the tie-breaker had dropped my weapon. My competitor had a clean performance, which relegated me to second place once again. This year I was not going to let that happen. The weapon I compete with is the cane (in Korean *Jee Pahng Ee*). I sat and visualized myself giving it my all, performing with grace, speed, and power. When it came time for the weapons portion, that's exactly the way it happened. That day I was to win my second World Championship outright with the cane. I was now a two-time World Champ. I was on cloud nine. By the time it came to the sparring portion of the competition, I was mentally, emotionally, and physically out of gas. I got knocked out in the first round, but I couldn't have been happier.

Saturday I took the day to savor my success by judging the young competitors portion of the new tournament cycle. Saturday young students from all over the world come to compete with the same hope: to one day be a World Champ. Adults begin the new tournament year by competing on Sunday. It is said that success is fleeting, and Sunday I got that memo. Maybe I was still enjoying my success too much. Maybe I was a little over confident. I can't rightly remember. That Sunday in forms, I came in second and, in weapons, I came in fourth. There's nothing like being brought down to earth, but I was still going home a World Champion and that's what I'd come to accomplish. Job well done.

Chief Master M.K. Lee awarding me my Gold Medal in forms

*Chief Master M.K. Lee with me;
over the years he has become a mentor and friend*

Holding my Gold Medal

CHAPTER 9
SCHOOL NUMBER TWO— GROWTH, SEPARATION AND THE PAIN OF EXPANSION

"Growth is the only guarantee that tomorrow is going to be better."

—*John Maxwell*

As the summer of 2008 moved into fall, we again experienced an influx of new students. By the end of October, we had eighty-five active students training regularly. Both my son and I were drawing a modest but regular salary, all the bills were being paid, and our savings account was growing. The coaches and courses we had been involved with over the last few years had definitely paid dividends; our marketing was producing results, our lead generation and conversions had improved, and we were on a solid footing. We had maintained a commercial presence in the community now for over four years. I felt that, after the initial challenges, we made some smart, prudent decisions. In the last four years, we had seen continued growth and development. We were also creating a growing status in the community. In January of 2009, we were nominated for our local Chamber of Commerce Outstanding Business of the Year Award for "Customer Excellence." It was the second year we had been nominated and that year we were to win. Our business was not only growing, we were being recognized by those in our community as well. It was a very satisfying feeling.

By the fall of 2008, I'd had time to consider the opportunity of opening a second location that had been offered to me in the summer. There was no doubt in my mind that, if we accepted it, my business acumen as well as my resiliency would be challenged.

The business next door was a music and dance school owned by an old business coach of ours, Sam. We had worked with him a year earlier, when our mentor was being coached by him, and we had a chance to hear Sam speak at one of our weekend retreats. As well, we had attended one of his weekend business seminars so we had some background with him. We've all heard the phrase "God moves in mysterious ways." Well, the opportunity to open our business right beside a music and dance studio would play a major role in the success of that location. At the time, I had no idea of its significance until a year after we had been in the space. The lessons learned from the opening of that school will go a long way the next time we expand.

In the early winter of 2008, after thoroughly thinking it over and talking about it with my son, we decided that, if the offer was genuine, we would commit to opening a second location there. We had done our due diligence and were confident we could make it work. We let Sam know that, if and when the space became available, we would be interested in taking it over. Robert would take over running of the White Rock School and I would run the King George School.

The arts are primarily a personality-driven business. Students and parents get attached to their instructor and vice versa. Once we had made the decision to open a second location, we began communicating to the students and parents that we were looking to expand within the next few months. I had heard from other instructors over my years in business that, when an established instructor leaves, it can have a negative impact on the existing student body. The transition from one instructor to a new one can really hurt the business. To mitigate the coming transition, Robert began teaching the majority of classes at the White Rock School while I worked in the back office.

MASTERSHIP

For the first five months of 2009, there was still nothing firm about if or when the new location would be vacated. February, March, April, and May all came and went with nothing changing, but eventually in June of 2009 I was informed that I could take possession August 1. On one hand, the wait had been easy as there was no pressure or solid commitment necessary. On the other hand, I had relaxed a bit as it had taken longer than anticipated to develop. As soon as I heard we had a firm possession date, I began to tighten up.

During the wait, I did what I could to prepare and plan how the process would go. I had ongoing discussions with the other instructor who wanted to come in as my partner, keeping him in the loop as things moved closer. In theory, everything would be straightforward, but now the die was cast and the rubber was about to hit the road. I was committed and, even with the planning and preparation work I'd done, I wasn't as sure of myself as I would have liked. Once again, I wondered if I was out of my depth.

In the winter of 2008, Carole and I had hoped to get away and spend a couple of weeks in Kailua-Kona on the big island of Hawaii, so I'd booked a condo for us. Unfortunately, Carole became quite sick that winter and we had to cancel our plans. Before she became ill, I'd put a deposit down on a condo. The owner said he would retain the deposit and I would be able to rebook as Carole's health improved.

Once I knew that we would be taking possession on August 1, I contacted the condo owner and asked if I could apply the money he had for a week sometime in July. I was lucky as there was a week available. Carole was still unable to fly due to her health issues, but she encouraged me to go. She knew that, once I took on the new location, there would be no chance of a break for quite a while and so I booked my flight. I thought this would be a good trip to prepare myself and get some rest and relaxation before taking possession. As it turned out, it wasn't quite the way I'd imagined it—you would think that, at sixty-one years of age, I would have learned by now. Upon arriving, I picked up my rental car and drove to the condo to get myself settled. Within a few hours, I was already unsettled. I was alone with my thoughts, didn't know a soul, had no one to talk to, and

I already missed Carole. So much for rest and relaxation. Many nights I woke up in a cold sweat, and believe me when I say that's hard to do in Kona in the middle of July. It's hot. Being alone with nothing but your thoughts for company can be challenging at the best of times, but when you're about to step into a new situation when you get home, my doubts and fears had a field day.

During the day, things weren't as bad, as I kept myself busy snorkeling and driving to Volcano Park and up to the north end of the island to take long hikes. These excursions kept me active and occupied, and freed from the thoughts that troubled me during the night. At night though, there was nothing to distract me. Many of those nights I didn't fare too well. Throughout my life, I have had times when I struggled greatly with my self-confidence to face down my fears. Yet knowing that has never stopped me from accepting challenges that gave rise to those same fears.

When I started my training at the Gateway Baptist Church back in 1996, Mr. Ford required us to memorize a motivational quote or a verse from the Bible to help internalize the life skill of that testing cycle. It would be directly related to the life skill we were working on. As a white belt, I memorized the verse Philippians 4:13. The verse spoke to me of hope and it gave me emotional strength. It is a verse that I study to this day as I always draw to it when I am troubled or feeling challenged. I'd brought my Bible to Kona and, one night when I was struggling with my internal dialogue; I started reading and found a passage in the book of Proverbs verse 16:3 that lifted my spirit: "Commit to the Lord whatever you do and your plans will succeed." Up to that point, everything I had done had been a commitment to God, so reading that verse was a gentle reminder to remain calm. Even today, when I read that verse, I remember that night in Kona and how much it helped.

Throughout my life, I have always had a spiritual leaning, even as a young boy. Though I've had my challenges with all organized branches of religion, it has never stopped me from drawing to and calling upon the higher power of God when in need. As I had progressed through the years of overcoming the frustration and disappointment of our bankruptcy, I found comfort in the readings from a variety of spiritual

MASTERSHIP

books. One of them was the Bible and another was the *Tao Te Ching* by Lao Tzu. Even though there were some enjoyable times during my stay in Kona (enjoyable enough that Carole and I now spend a couple of weeks there every winter), I was really glad to board the plane and get back home. Why? Simply because at home I could do something: I could get back to work. That's exactly what I did.

Before I'd left, I had made the commitment: I had signed a five-year lease and negotiated to pay the common costs for the first three months. I would take care of all the leasehold improvements. Full rent would kick in November 1 and, as with the White Rock School, my goal was to enroll enough students to be able to cover the rent by then. There was one major difference this time: I was starting from scratch. I would have no students to begin with, which meant no income until students enrolled. Today I would do things differently, but at that time, I decided that all classes would be for white belts. I didn't let any of the existing White Rock students come there to train. In hindsight, that was a mistake for a number of reasons, but that's the way we learn. Bruce Lee once said, "Mistakes are forgivable if one has the courage to admit them." Where would you like me to start?

> **"Mistakes are forgivable if one has the courage to admit them."**
> **—Bruce Lee**

Once I had taken possession on August 1, I had no choice but to follow through. The first things that needed to be done were to immediately clean it up and purchase and put down a new training floor. My goal was to be open by the third week of August, just before the kids went back to school. I got to work cleaning the space up, ordering the new training floor, setting up the reception area, and getting things ready to go. Opening before school officially returned was important for me, as I intended to have new students on the floor training by September, when things would get busy. As the school came together, the last piece being the installation of the training floor, I felt cautiously optimistic. However, that optimism was about to take a big hit.

Two things were about to happen before I even had a chance to officially open. They set my challenge bar so high that I don't know why I simply didn't just collapse into a fetal position and stay there. What made matters worse was they both happened within hours of each other on the same day. That day just happened to be my sixty-second birthday.

The first happened when Robert and I went home for lunch. My wife, Carole, had been dealing with severe mental health issues for many years and they had taken their toll on her and on our relationship. I didn't realize how much until that day. As we were sitting down to eat lunch, Carole said she had something to tell Robert and me. Sitting us down, she said she had decided to leave and live closer to her sister in a small town in the interior of BC called Logan Lake. It hit both of us like a bombshell, but for me it was devastating. I had not seen this coming at all and, as Robert told me later, neither had he. We had been married twenty-nine years and had always let each other know what was going on; not this time.

The day before, we had held a family get-together with our three children to celebrate my birthday and everything was as normal as ever. Now, all of a sudden, here she was informing us that she was leaving. There was to be no discussion. She told us that her sister and husband would be coming down the following weekend to pick her up and move her to Logan Lake. Robert and I were caught unawares. In our twenty-nine years together, Carole and I had been through some pretty tough times and we had overcome all those challenges together. She was my heart and soul, but she was now telling me it was over and she was leaving. I was struck dumb, lost for words. I tried to comprehend what was taking place and why, but couldn't quite get a grip on it all. I didn't know what to do. I wanted to work it through, but Carole told me there was no point; she had made her decision. I knew I had to get back to the new school as there was still work to be completed, but at that moment nothing was making sense. When I left, we agreed to talk more about it that evening, but her decision was final. I left our home with as heavy a heart as I've ever known, as I'm sure my son did as well.

On the drive over to the school, my mind raced over what had just taken place. Where had this decision come from? What had precipitated it? There were no indications, no talk, and no discussion; there was nothing to suggest that this decision was even in the works. Over the previous years with Carole's stays in the hospital, I had done everything I could think of to keep our home a peaceful and secure place of refuge. There's no denying that there were times that, due to concerns for her and the business, I definitely wasn't at my best. Through all those times, there was never any talk or the slightest indication of separating or splitting up. In that moment, I was at a total loss for an answer, but as she said, it was a done deal and I/we had to accept it.

Upon arriving at the King George location, I set to work but struggled to find my focus. I was totally at loose ends, stumbling around trying to compose myself, when my cell rang. It was my future partner, who had committed to opening this school with me. We had not put anything down in writing but had given each other our word, which for me was all I needed. I guess by now you know what's coming. Yes, he was phoning me to tell me that he didn't think he was up to helping me run a commercial operation. "Really?!" I said. "Everything pretty much ready to go, and all you're responsible for is teaching classes on a daily basis and shadowing me to learn how a commercial business runs, and you're pulling out now, a week before I wanted to open." What in God's name was I going to do? I had committed to five years, and landlords, even if you know them, don't take kindly to you backing out on a signed agreement. After hanging up I just sat there, not knowing whether to laugh or cry. In less than two hours, my wife had told me she was leaving and my future partner had backed out. What was left? If I thought I felt lost before, I was nowhere to be found now. Somehow, I had to pick myself up. Somehow, I had to move forward. There was no other choice; it was the only way to go. As much as I remember the day I found the $1,111 on the floor of the White Rock School, I also remember the day of my sixty-second birthday as well. I didn't know where to go or what to do, so I simply went home.

For me, one of the saving graces of taekwondo during times that have been challenging is the dedication and discipline to my daily training regimen. Over the next few months, it would again give me a focus and reason to get up. It brought a little peace every day and

I cherished the time to work on the patterns or hit the bags; getting the endorphins and dopamine flowing has always lifted my spirits.

During the next few weeks, other than the opening of the King George School, I had to come to terms with my new reality. As Carole stated, her sister and husband came down the following weekend to pick her up along with her belongings. I opened the new location as planned, without the other instructor, and I was now responsible for the mortgage on our home, the challenges of opening and growing a new location, and soon we'd be dealing with the fallout from a segment of the parent group from the White Rock school who were unhappy with the change. Oh, happy day.

Grand Master Emeritus Soon Ho Lee and me after a training session

MASTERSHIP

A group of black belt graduates; ceremony held at the King George school

CHAPTER 10
CHALLENGES

"That which does not kill us makes us stronger."
—*Friedrich Nietzsche*

Even though my son, Robert, had been the primary instructor at the White Rock School for several months, problems arose when I permanently made the move to the new location. I had been at the school most of the time, but I was usually in the back office working. I was always available to assist in class if the need arose, but I wanted Robert to build and establish a bond with the students and parents. We had made a point of communicating over the preceding months that we were expanding. We had done this through as many mediums as we could think of, before and during class, at testing's, and through emails. When the move actually took place, though, there was push back from some of the parents and students.

A percentage of our existing student base wanted to continue to train with me at the new location. The King George School was only a five-minute drive from White Rock. The only problem with that was I had not planned class times for anyone but white belts, tigers, kids, teens, and adults; this was an error on my part. Not

"Sometimes you win, sometimes you learn."
—John Maxwell

being able to train with me created some challenges as martial arts can be very personality driven. Students and parents form a relationship with their instructors. As a result, we lost some of our students due to this decision. You've heard the saying "hindsight is 20/20." In the future, when I do it again, I will definitely do it differently. I will plan better and make sure to create time and classes for those students wishing to continue training with whichever instructor they choose. Over the next couple of months, we were able to calm the waters and keep moving forward. I did what I thought best at the time and as John Maxwell says, "Sometimes you win, sometimes you learn." I definitely learned a great deal from that experience, from a business, personal, and emotional perspective.

Going into business beside a music and dance school was a blessing in disguise that I had not anticipated, something I would come to appreciate, especially over the next six months and over the years that followed. It was the best business and marketing move we've ever unwittingly made; all I did was open next door. Our two businesses served the same demographic. In the years that we've been there, we have enrolled a great many students simply because we were right next door. When mom or dad, usually mom, brings one of their children to sign up for dance or music lessons, more often than not the sibling is brought over to us and enrolled in martial arts. Our businesses benefited each other and the location would definitely become a boon for ours. However, once again it would take longer in developing than I anticipated.

As with a great many things I've done in my life, I overestimated how simple things were going to be and underestimated how hard. I'd made a similar mistake when I opened the White Rock School five years earlier. It was to be no different here. Once again, I misjudged how long it would take to get to the breakeven point. Having had a previous relationship with the owner of the business was to quickly become a saving grace as Sam was willing to work with me while I got the location up and running. From his perspective, I think it was easier to help me get established than to ask me to leave and then spend months trying to lease the space. It was my $1,111 in a different form.

As mentioned earlier, Sam and I had met through one of my business coaches a couple of years back. I'd met Sam at a weekend seminar put on by my coach, and Sam had invited everyone there (at a rather substantial but reduced fee—$5,000 down to $3,000) to attend a weekend seminar he was putting on. That was a year I would spend a significant amount of money on business coaching and marketing development. Searching out different coaches and mentors is essential to improving one's business or life development. I love sports, and all players at any level need coaches if they are going to improve. For me it was no different in business, especially if I wanted to stay in the game, and I did. If I recognized an area in which I was weak, I would then start looking for a coach who could give me some insight and guidance. The challenging part of this procedure was finding someone I trusted who aligned with our thinking while, at the same time, challenged me to think outside the box. This was not always easy.

One key factor I've learned over my years in business is that it's not all about what you know, but also about who you know. You can then develop a respectful working relationship with them. We just never know when or where we might meet someone who, in the future, we might be able to help. This was the case with Sam.

Sam took a chance with me, for which I am grateful. In the first few months of my five-year lease, he was willing to work with me through the rough times when I was unable to pay full rent. He did this by extending the partial lease payments beyond the agreed upon date by a few months, which gave me a little more time to get the location to a point of liquidity. His patience and belief in me paid off as over the years it developed into a win-win situation. He now has a solid, stable tenant and I have a successful business. Oh, those extra months of partial payments that he extended to me at the beginning of the lease I am presently repaying him. In business, nothing is ever free.

By March 1 of 2010, the King George location finally got to the breakeven point, and the White Rock location had stabilized and was growing again. I was beginning to settle into my new reality. Carole had been in Logan Lake for seven months. She had found a condo and was living close to her sister. Robert and I were continuing to focus on improving our business acumen through courses and coaches, and my life had settled into a calmer daily routine, which was nice. All the business training that we'd taken over the last few years would continue to pay dividends by creating the growth and income that would allow us to expand our instructor pool.

As 2010 rolled into 2011, the King George School began enrolling students on a consistent basis, and we were pushing ninety for the active student base of the White Rock School. Being located next to the music and dance studio had created a problem that I had not dealt with in White Rock: walk-ins. For the first two years, I was the only instructor on the floor with no one to help when someone would walk in. Because of where the White Rock School was located, we seldom if ever had a walk-in. This situation definitely began creating challenges for me. When someone would walk in, I would want to be able to greet them, but that would mean I'd have to leave the training floor to do that. Over time, I became pretty proficient at handling the people who walked in, getting their name, number, and the best time to call without taking too much time away from the training floor. However, by the end of the day, I would be exhausted.

In all my business training, I came to realize the one major area that had not ever been covered was human resources. Up to this point, it had only been my son and I running each location. I didn't have any experience in how to go about hiring someone. What do you look for? What would be their job description? How much would you pay them beyond minimum wage? How many hours a week would I need them to work? Even though we now have a staff, it's still probably my weakest area. Both schools were growing beyond what either of us was responsibly capable of handling on our own. It was starting to become a growing concern and a bit overwhelming.

My son and I put a lot of effort into building relationships with our students and their families. As the schools grew, we found we had less time to spend on those essential bonds. I felt it was beginning to hurt our ability to connect with them. By June of 2011, we knew we had to do something but were at a loss as to what. In Songahm Taekwondo, you just can't hire an instructor off the street and train him or her quickly.

To become a certified instructor takes a minimum of two years of study and training. There are tests and requirements that must be met and passed before certification. As well, all candidates must have and maintain clear criminal records. At that time, we didn't have anyone in our student body pipeline. Truth be told, we didn't have a pipeline at all, nor did we know anyone in any of the other schools in the area who we might approach. We were at a standstill. There didn't seem to be many options and we weren't even sure where to begin. Queue another fortuitous moment.

At the beginning of July in the summer of 2011 as I was going through my daily emails, I noticed a résumé come in from a local instructor trained in Songahm Taekwondo. I knew this instructor. Ben had sent out his résumé, looking for full time work.

In Songahm, all instructors must be certified by our organization. Once an instructor becomes certified, they generally stay and work for their instructor or they open their own school. At that time Ben was working part time in three different schools and was hoping to find full time work in one. I had met him over the years at various regional tournaments and testing's, so I knew who he was. I immediately contacted him and we set a time to meet. After a couple of meetings, I quickly realized he had a skill set that covered an area of our business my son and I struggled with: making cold calls and setting appointments.

We had binders full of leads that we had accumulated over the last couple of years from doing every community event we could find. At each event, we would put up a tent and table with information about our schools and locations. Parents and children passing by would be encouraged to come over and spin our prize wheel to win anything from a free birthday party to the top prize of six months of free lessons and a uniform. To be able to spin the wheel, they would have to give us some personal information—name, address, phone number, etc.—so we could contact them to set up an appointment for them to come in and redeem their prize. Over the years, we had done so many events and collected so much information and tried to make all the call backs, but if we got an answering machine, which was the general rule, we left messages and moved on with no follow-up. So we had all these binders full of names and numbers with the prizes won notated on each page. It was a gold mine waiting to be worked; we needed a miner.

Making cold calls and doing it well is to my mind a special ability, and neither my son nor I were good at it. We could field incoming calls relatively well, but cold calls not so much. Ben could definitely benefit the company; as there was enough available work for him to do that, he could get started immediately.

That being said, the next challenge would be financial. Could we afford to pay him? Robert and I had worked our way to a decent salary; in that regard, I hadn't really had much choice. When Carole left, I became solely responsible for the mortgage on our condo, as well as all the bills. After discussing the matter between the three of us, we came to a workable agreement. Ben would continue to work the three jobs he had presently over July and August. He would also work for us two hours in the morning, three to four days a week, depending on his schedule, doing cold calls. We would pay him an hourly rate.

If, through the appointments he made from his cold calls, we were able to enroll twenty new students over the summer months, then come September we would hire him full time. The twenty new students would cover his salary and not draw down on our existing bottom line. As he worked his way through our cold call binders, we experienced continued growth. Come September, we had enrolled thirty new students over those two months, so we were ahead of the game. As of September 1, 2011, Ben came to work for us as a full time instructor/employee. Over the years, he has become a stable member of our company. He continues to make calls today and for the first few years he also enrolled new students. It was definitely a win-win situation. Ben had a full time job and stability, and we gained not only an instructor but also an employee with a skill set that strengthened the company.

By 2013, the King George location had grown to 140 active students, with Ben and me teaching classes and enrolling new students regularly. The White Rock School was holding steady at sixty active students, but the numbers had dropped off considerably because of a complete loss of available parking. This was due to the construction of a low-rise literally twenty feet from our front door.

MASTERSHIP

In the fall of that year, we had the opportunity to hire another certified Songahm instructor, Matt. He was a young man in his early twenties and we thought he would be a good fit to work with Robert at the White Rock School. Our hope was that, between the two of them, we could get White Rock back on its feet. Even though I seriously questioned whether we could really afford the extra salary, we decided to go ahead. Matt was a detailed-orientated instructor who worked well with all our students, young and old. He would also be able to help Robert in our marketing and by submitting our testing results to HQ, thus helping decrease some of Robert's workload. Now we had four certified instructors, all with valuable yet different skill sets that could assist in moving the company forward. We had taken another step in our business.

Robert and I had come quite a ways in the last nine years and overcome more than a few challenges along the way. With Ben and Matt, the company was looking stronger than ever. My role changed a bit; I didn't have to be on the floor as much and could work on the business a little more and not in it as much. I still enjoyed teaching as much as ever, but I came to realize it's not about me, it's about we, and my role was to lead the company forward.

It's not about me, it's about we, and my role was to lead the company forward

Becoming an employer was not something I had ever envisioned back in 2004. I had simply wanted to find a way to share the benefits of Songahm with as many people as I could reach. In 2010, one of our parents shared a book with me called *Mastering the Rockefeller Habits* by Verne Harnish. One of the key things that resonated with me from reading the book was defining our purpose and delineating our "core values." It took me a good couple of months to distill these two aspects of the business. Our purpose I define as "creating a positive life-altering option for our students, families and community" and our core values are "relentless," "resilient," "continuous improvement and development," and "health and fitness." As we grew and evolved into a company, these concepts were needed to create a consistent thread between the entire staff and any future staff we hired.

Throughout 2011 and 2012, with Ben and me working at the King George School, our enrollment and upgrade numbers began to climb. By mid-2012, we were pushing 130 active students and the days of financial uncertainty were in the past. The White Rock School, as mentioned, had taken a hit starting in the summer of 2010. In the early spring, we had just signed a new five-year lease. Within months of the signing, we were to lose over ninety-five percent of our parking and our ease of access. Since taking possession six years before, we had been aware of the potential of this happening. We knew that the lots and buildings adjacent to us had been sold and there had been rumors for years that they were scheduled for demolition and development. This had been continually put off over the last few years due to the downturn in the economy. So we were surprised when, one June morning in 2010, we arrived at the school to find blue safety fencing twenty-five feet from our front door and the access to our parking completely cut off. This left only a small twenty-foot wide laneway, which would allow four cars max for our students and staff to park.

This was going to be only the beginning. For the next three years, we dealt with construction issues from the flooding of the entrance to our business due to the construction blocking off what used to be a natural run-off for rainwater. On the West Coast of Canada, we can get a lot of rain in a very short period in the winter. The contractors assumed they could access the construction site through what little property we had left and at times took up the remaining parking. That blocked access to the entrance to our business. Other times, there would be nails all over the entrance to the school, which punctured customers' tires. For three years, it was an ongoing battle with continual, almost daily disruption to our business. There were days I would be on the phone to our building's management relaying what was taking place and needing them to contact the construction company to get these issues resolved. It was a struggle to keep sixty students actively training. I give a lot of credit and thanks to the students and parents who stayed with us and continued their training under such conditions.

My son, Robert, worked tirelessly to ensure the best possible training for those students. It's to his credit that the White Rock School is still in operation today.

One of the main reasons we hired Matt in 2013 was to allow Robert some time away from teaching all the classes. Matt also brought some fresh ideas regarding how we could improve our marketing and would be a great help to Robert in that area. The time away from the training floor would also allow Robert time to continue to work on systems development as well as some strategies for our marketing. Having taken on another salary, and with the completion of the building next door, our priority became getting White Rock healthy again. When we first opened the King George School, the White Rock School had carried it until it could pay for itself. For two years, it had been the reverse, with King George picking up the slack for White Rock. It was time to get both schools back on an equal footing and into the black.

This may sound naïve or idealistic, but I did not go into business thinking it was a great way to make money as mentioned earlier, that was never my driving force. Though, I quickly realized I had to make money to stay in business. To this day, making money is not a motivating factor. Giving people the opportunity to change their lives is key for me, and to do that I needed to be a good steward of the money we brought in.

With the firsthand experience I'd had on the benefits that training in Songahm Taekwondo can bring to one's life, sharing that positive life-altering option has been my purpose. I knew what it did for me and somehow I had to find a way to share that experience with others. The only way I could think of was to teach and reach out to as many people as I could. I believe so strongly in the positive effects of Songahm Taekwondo that I would gladly teach it at no charge. The funny thing is that the people who have said they could definitely see the benefits but couldn't really afford it seldom stayed the course, no matter what I did. I've extended a hand to help many times throughout my years through reduced monthly fees and other accommodations, but most have never seen their training through to completion; somewhere along the line they quit.

Over the years, I've concluded that it is seldom a money problem. Most of the time, it's an attitude problem regarding value. Let me give you an example. When I first opened the White Rock School, I had a special needs child named Tamara, who was enrolled by her special needs single parent named Wendy. Wendy could have spent what little money she made doing menial labour jobs and what she received monthly from the government on many things. She chose, though, to enroll her daughter with me. Tamara trained with me from 2002, when I first began teaching at the White Rock club, until 2009. During that time, I never once had to follow up with Wendy regarding her monthly tuition. Wendy told me many times of the value Tamara received in her training. Her daughter was more valuable than money, so it never became an issue. In fact, when money was tight, Wendy would always come to me, and we would put a plan in place until she could take care of it, which she always did. It seems to me that, in our culture, if we don't have to pay for something, we don't place any value in what we receive.

I've learned many valuable life lessons on this journey in my second life. Honor and integrity are two of them. I believe these two life skills have played a major role in the success of our business. For me, honor is what I've received by being invited into a family's or student's life. When they enroll in our school, they give me the chance to share with them the benefits of Songahm and that to me is a special privilege. I am humbled and honored when I meet them out in the community and they refer to me as Mr. Davidson. When it comes to integrity, the phrase I remember is "doing the right thing even when no one is watching"; for me, there is always someone watching or aware of my actions. I have made many mistakes and errors in my life and in our business, but I've done my best to own every one. In my world, that's the way I build integrity.

After signing the White Rock lease, there was never a question about trying to find a way out of it. The problem became how we were going to make it work for us and work our way through it. We kept to this focus despite feeling mislead by our landlord, as shortly after having us sign the lease, the building was sold. When selling commercial property, it always helps to sell a building with a long-term tenant locked in. Even through all the challenges that the next three years were to bring, I chose to live up to my commitment. For me, it was simply a matter of integrity—nothing more, nothing less. I'd signed the contract and that was all there was to it.

After 2013, when the building next door was completed and the construction problems were over, we were still left with no available parking for our students. This was no longer a tenable situation. As our lease was expiring, we went looking for a new location and were fortunate to find one right around the corner—no more than a one-minute walk. We could not have asked for more. It was located in a small strip mall right down the street. We would lose some square footage, but the new space was wide open, other than washrooms, so we would be able to design a complete build-out. We had never had the opportunity to do that before. This would be a new experience. The new location also allowed us greater visibility with lots of parking and easier access for our appreciative students and parents.

It seems that, for every decision and action I make, as much as I think I have covered all the bases, life will show me that I still have more learning to do. This would be the case with the new location. With the White Rock School, we started with a $9,000 capital investment. With the King George School, since it had previously been a martial arts school when we took possession, there was an initial capital investment of approximately $5,000 for the training floor and painting.

With the new White Rock location, it would be a complete build-out. Upon taking possession on January 1, 2015, we would have sixty days to do a complete build-out and be ready to open our doors on March 1, which was when the old lease expired. I had received accurate dimensions from our new landlord and had designed a floor plan that had a decent office and intro room. I then took the design to a professional to have a proper floor plan created and brought those plans to City Hall to be approved for a building permit, which we needed to get started. Compared to the old location, we would be losing about eight hundred square feet. The important thing, though, would be that the training floor square footage would remain pretty much the same. The old location, although bigger, had space that we could never use effectively; we had been paying for space we didn't use. In the new location, we would use every inch effectively. A week before we were to open, we were given our final approval, allowing us to officially move our business to the newly renovated location and open as planned on March 1.

Over those sixty days, I learned a great deal about dealing with City Hall and building permits, building codes, and final approvals, along with the finer points of plumbing, heating, and electrical issues. Overall, everything worked out pretty much as we had hoped. In all, the work took approximately six weeks to complete, and after receiving our final approval, we opened on schedule to a very appreciative student and parent body.

The location and layout was definitely a step up from the previous one, but for one issue: heat. My inexperience in negotiations would come back to haunt me on that issue. The new location had four large single-pane glass windows, two in front facing the street and two in back facing the parking lot. They pretty much went from floor to ceiling, which was about thirteen feet high. This is great for visibility, but in the winter, the windows are a tremendous source of heat loss. We found out the space was incredibly hard to heat. The landlord had been unwilling to install a HVAC system, so my next option was to speak to the electrical contractor we'd hired during the build-out about what options we might have. We ended up installing electric baseboard heaters and a couple of small entrance way furnaces. We found out quickly in our first winter that what we had installed was not adequate to heat the space. We then added some smaller radiant ceiling heaters, which helped, but with the high ceiling, keeping the place warm in the winter was challenging. The winter of 2016 was even colder, so unless we can get this issue resolved, we will be moving when our lease runs out in three years. As they say, "live and learn." Since we have three years left on both leases, our goal is to purchase either a strata space or a small building in our community and amalgamate the two schools.

MASTERSHIP

By 2016, we had come so much further than I ever could have imagined in my wildest dreams when I purchased the club from Mr. Ford in 2002. Along the journey, I learned more about myself and business than I ever could have conceived possible. There will always be issues to deal with, such as the heating in the new school, but the upgrade in the change of venue far outweighed the problems. Our business was doing well and I was doing what I'd set out to do: share the benefits and follow the vision of Eternal Grand Master.

Always working and training, improving myself mentally and physically, no matter what the challenge was in front of me

CHAPTER 11
REUNITED

"Being deeply loved by someone gives you strength, while loving someone deeply gives you courage."

—*Lao Tzu*

On August 22, 2009, my heart and soul walked out our front door. We had been married twenty-nine years. I was devastated. I felt lost and had no anchor. We had been through some challenging times as a couple and as a family, but we had always been able to work through it together. Carole leaving tore me up, and shocked and hurt our children. By 2009, she had been battling her demons for over fifteen years. The first time I was truly aware of the depth of her pain and horror was in the summer of 1994; we'd been married fourteen years. I remember the moment that changed our lives ever so clearly. We had just taken Kat, Robyn, and Robert out to stay with Carole's mom in Alberta for a few weeks, so it was just the two of us at home. One night, Carole was in the basement ironing some clothes. I had just started walking up the stairs to go do something when she said, "Why did they let him do that to me?"

I stopped and said, "Who? What?"

"My grandfather."

"What are you talking about?" I asked. "What did your grandfather do to you and who let him?"

"Why did my mom and grandmother let him abuse me? They let him abuse me from the time I was a baby until I was well into my teens."

I was dumbstruck and didn't know what to say. After fourteen years of marriage, I was hearing about this for the first time. I had been aware that there were some issues with her family. I knew I had never liked the way they treated her, but I had no idea how deep the issue was. In looking back now, I believe that the love and trust we'd developed for each other over the years of our marriage had somehow allowed her to trust me with these memories. There always seemed to be a secretive atmosphere around her family. Things were kept quiet and not spoken of. Until that moment, I don't think Carole had wanted to face that ugly truth or verbalize it. When those nine words tumbled out of her mouth, it irrevocably changed the course of our lives and marriage forever. It would start Carole on a self-destructive/healing path that to this day continues to affect all our lives. Over the coming years, there would be periods of deep depression combined with self-harm and periods where, through medication and medical support, Carole would appear to be on the way to better health. Carole has always been a fighter, and now she was in a fight for her sanity and her life.

Over the next fifteen years, the memories of what she endured for the first seventeen years of her life would rip at her daily. They would also put enormous pressure on our marriage and affect our family in a multitude of ways. The memories from her abused childhood wreaked havoc on her mind, body, and spirit. Her life became a gradually worsening existence that would be punctuated by periods where she seemed able to come to terms with it. Then, the next bout of depression and anxiety would become deeper and more pronounced, worse than the time before. Many times she would have suicidal thoughts and erratic behavior, so much so that often she would have to be admitted to the hospital and spend time in the psychiatric ward. The times spent in the hospital could vary from days, weeks, or months, depending on the severity of her depression.

MASTERSHIP

Many times, Carole was aware enough of what was happening that she would request admittance. One time though, my son and I had to literally carry her into the hospital in a catatonic state and watch as the hospital staff stuck pins in the bottom of her feet to see if she would respond, which she didn't. That night, the only thing we could do was kiss her goodbye and go home. The next day when I visited her, she had regained consciousness and was in a holding room that was completely devoid of anything but Carole and a mat to lie on. She barely knew me. I thank God that only happened once, but she remained in the hospital for well over a month that time, before being able to come home. During one of her stays, she was administered electric shock treatment over a period of weeks. These treatments would affect many areas of her memory and ability to do simple math. I cannot even begin to imagine the horrors she endured as a child growing up that would cause such a trauma to her soul. I've lived with and watched the repercussions of those events play out daily for more than twenty years.

The one saving grace with her stays in the hospital was that the hospital was a three-block walk from our home and located on the route I took home from the King George School. This allowed both Robert and me the ability to visit her pretty much every day she was there. It wasn't much, but she always had one or both of us come in and give her some love and support.

Since I first met Carole, she had always been conscious of and concerned about what she put in her body in terms of food, drink, and medicine. It is because of her that I have become so much more conscious and knowledgeable about what foods are healthy. She's the reason I have become much more disciplined about what I put into my body. Food has become fuel for me. Over the years of dealing with her depression and demons, I became more concerned about her when she would come home from the hospital with a new prescription, or three. Most of them were on a trial basis to see how her mind and body would react, which to me was basically taking a shot in the dark. As her hospital stays increased, so did the frequency of new and different medicines.

This was not the woman I'd married. The health and vibrancy of the person I had met back in 1980 were slowly slipping away. Between 2005 and 2008, stays in the hospital became common place as she slipped deeper into her personal hell. In the latter part of 2008, things appeared to be improving. Carole seemed to have stabilized and her mental, emotional, and physical health had improved. By the summer of 2009, she did not feel the need to go back into the hospital other than to see her psychiatrist, who she saw on a weekly basis for many months and continues seeing to this day. Things seemed to be stabilizing until August 17, 2009, when the bottom fell out of my world.

When Carole moved out, it became a reckoning for me. Even during her darkest moments, she had always been there and I was able to do whatever I could to help her. Now she was gone and I couldn't be there for her if she needed me, or if I needed her. There was some peace of mind for me in that she would be living close to her sister, who was a pharmacist and would be able to help her if she needed it, someone who would be there if she started to spiral down again. But it was something I had to learn to deal with.

One of the positive things the separation did was to allow me uninterrupted time to focus on the business. I threw myself fully into it without being split between the businesses and wondering how Carole was doing on a daily basis. Over that winter, I settled into this new reality and Carole settled into hers in Logan Lake. She had been able to find a nice one-bedroom apartment, move in with the help of her sister and brother-in-law in September, and set herself up. We had little communication over the next few months and, although I missed her, I was happy for her. What little communication I did receive from her seemed to indicate she was stable and comfortable. I also wanted to make sure I gave her the space she wanted. With her sister's help, she would drive to Kamloops on a regular basis about forty-five minutes away to see a doctor who had been recommended by her psychiatrist here at home. This also helped to put my mind at rest.

By the spring of the following year, we had re-established a comfortable line of communication. If this was the way it was to be, I discussed with Carole, then I thought it only right that she owned her own place as well, since I was in our home. In going forward, I wanted to make sure we both had a home of our own.

The home in White Rock would always be ours, but if this was what she wanted, I did not want her renting. In our brief communications, she told me that she was comfortable for the most part with where she was. She had her good days and bad days, but overall she was good. She mentioned in one of our conversations that the apartment she was in was for sale, so I asked her if she was up to looking into the price. She said she was, and I told her if she wanted the condo, I would find a mortgage broker here to figure out how to restructure our existing mortgage and free up some money for the necessary down payment. We both did our jobs and by late February of 2010 we had everything in place and were able to purchase the condo for her. That felt good.

Having her own home was important as was the understanding that her decision to leave did not stop me loving her. After everything was signed and she had her own home, things began to improve between us, not only in our communications but in our overall relationship. In the late spring of 2010, when I could get away from the school on the weekends, I would make the three-hour drive to Logan Lake and we would spend the weekend together. In some ways, it was like when we first met. One of the things that had attracted me to Carole was that she was one person I could be completely open and honest with about anything. I didn't have to couch what I said and could just say what was on my mind or in my heart. She took it all in stride without becoming offended, hurt, or angry. I had never met anyone like that and, even though that part of our relationship had deteriorated over the years, for the most part we were still comfortable speaking what was on our minds without it turning into a fight.

In fact, in our twenty-nine years of marriage, I think I could count the number of times we really argued on one hand and, even then, we'd end up either laughing or apologizing to each other by the end of it all. We loved each other and we respected each other's right to their own opinion, even when we disagreed. Over the summer and fall of 2010, we spent a lot of weekends together and for Christmas that year the kids and I all drove up to Logan Lake and spent the holidays with

Mom in her one-bedroom home. It was like being on the road again when we were playing music, all of us in a hotel room, except now the kids were all adults and Kat had been able to bring Aria as well. As crowded as it was, it was good to have our family together again.

I don't remember exactly when, during Carole's time there, her mother moved out from Alberta and took up residence in Merritt, which is a small community about a thirty-minute drive from Logan Lake. Her mom made the move so she could be closer to her two daughters. It turned out fortuitously, as shortly after the move her mom was diagnosed with cancer. It fell to Carole to become her caregiver and drive her to her various appointments and treatments. To get her mom to her appointments was usually a ninety-minute drive each way over a high mountain pass. During the summer, this wasn't a serious problem, although the physical and emotional strain on Carole was considerable. In the winter, however, the pass became more than treacherous. In the mountains, you can start out driving under clear skies and drive straight into white-out conditions where it's snowing so hard and heavy you struggle to see past the hood of your car. You can literally drive off the road without even seeing it coming. Over the winter of 2010, Carole had to make that harrowing trip more times than she would have liked. It took a serious toll on her fragile health, but it was something she felt she needed to do.

There were times when Carole would also have to drive down to our White Rock home every so often to see her psychiatrist and then turn around and drive home a day or two later after resting up. On one of her return trips over a different mountain pass, I received a call from her mother asking me if I'd heard from Carole. She wanted to find out what time she had left as she hadn't checked in on her way home and it was getting dark. Winter driving in the mountains only gets worse as night sets in. I told her what time Carole had left, but I hadn't heard anything from her since. Within the hour, I received another call from her mom telling me that the police had just brought Carole to her place. She had hit black ice and rolled her vehicle multiple times, landing in the median between the two highways. The car was totaled and she was lucky to be alive and, even luckier, relatively unhurt. Of all the things in the car that day, the only thing that survived that accident besides Carole was a framed picture of my mom, who had passed away a few months earlier. Nothing else was recovered. Carole would tell me later that she felt Mom had been with her that day. Over the twenty plus years of travelling on the road when we were playing music, we had witnessed many fatal and near-fatal accidents on both those mountain passes, so we were blessed that Carole survived that day.

In the spring of 2011, her mother's condition began to deteriorate and it was recommended that she move to Vancouver to receive better treatment. From 2009 to the early part of 2011, Carole and I were able to slowly re-establish our relationship; the period of separation had been beneficial for both of us. Robert and I had been able to build our business and become more self-reliant and the time on her own had helped Carole learn to cope better with her demons. After she had recovered from the accident and the snow and ice left the mountain passes, Carole moved her mom to a respite care facility in the White Rock area. She then asked me if she could move home, to which I gladly agreed.

Carole and me dancing at our daughter Robyn's wedding in December 2014

CHAPTER 12
ONWARD AND UPWARD

"New occasions teach new duties."
—*James Russell Lowell*

I always remember my mom saying to me as I was growing up, especially when things got tough, that "the hardest part of every race is the last hundred yards." For the next five years of my journey, I would be reminded of this phrase more than a few times.

After reuniting with the love of my life in the spring of 2011, I headed for Little Rock, Arkansas. On June 24, 2011, I successfully tested for my fifth degree black belt. I was still on track. At a leadership summit held a couple years earlier, we had been asked by Grand Master if we had set a goal for when we planned to test for our sixth degree black belt and begin our training for Mastership. I had set my goal for June 2016 for the sixth degree and June 2017 to be inducted as a Master.

In Songahm Taekwondo, for every rank of black belt we hold, we must train for a minimum of that many years. For me to be able to test for my sixth degree in June 2016, I had to successfully test in June of 2011 for my fifth degree—and I had. Little did I know at the time that I was about to start on the most challenging, disappointing, grueling, but ultimately successful part of my martial arts journey. During our time in rank, we had to successfully pass three mid-terms to be eligible to test up to the next rank. As a fifth degree, these could only be done at a national event like the Spring Nationals in Las Vegas, Worlds in Little Rock, Fall Nationals in Orlando, or internationally in Korea. The best score we could hope to achieve was ten points, based on five points for our form (*poome-sae*), three points for sparring (*gyeo-roo-gi*), and two points for our board breaks, if we broke all stations the first time. As a fifth degree, I was required to break boards with two hand techniques and two foot techniques. If I completed breaking all the stations on my second or third attempts, I'd receive a single point, and if I did not break one or more stations on my third attempt, I would receive zero for my final board score.

Up to this point, I had done thirteen mid-terms and four rank tests since achieving my first degree. During that time, only once did I not achieve a passing score. That was all about to change. From first to third degree, to successfully pass a mid-term or rank testing, a student had to achieve a minimum score of seven out of ten. Once a student achieves their fourth degree, they are required to score eight out of ten, which doesn't leave much wiggle room. During my time in fourth degree, a fit test was introduced as part of our testing requirements. It is composed of five components: thirty push-ups; fifty sit-ups; a six-kick combination done ten times (sixty kicks); a jab, cross punch, round kick combination done off both sides ten times (sixty techniques in total); and a ten-punch boxing combination done ten times, for a total of three hundred techniques. Other than the push-ups and sit-ups, we were hitting bags and being graded on the effort, speed, and power of our techniques. We were also being timed, from ages 17–39, we have five minutes to complete the three hundred techniques, from 40–59 we have six minutes, and for 60 and up, we have seven minutes. When the fit test was first introduced, we had to successfully complete it once a year. Now a student must successfully complete it at every mid-term or rank test at a regional or national event. The fit test is generally done after we've completed our testing and, as mentioned earlier, we are graded on our effort. If the effort is poor, we can receive negative one point, which would be deducted from our final testing score. If it's adequate we receive zero extra points, leaving our final testing score unchanged and, if we bust a gut and go all out, we can receive one extra point to our score. This gives us a chance to improve our final score if we think we need it.

The only time the fit test was not required during my time in fifth degree was when I travelled to Korea. Every two to three years, our organization organizes a ten-day trip to Korea. In 2011 there was a trip planned but I was unable to go but I promised myself that when the next time a trip to Korea came up, I would go. That opportunity came in April of 2013 and, combined with the trip, was an opportunity to do my first mid-term as a fifth degree. I was now sixty-six years old, the schools were doing well, and I had the staff to cover my absence. As soon as I decided to go, I began to prepare myself mentally and physically for the trip and test. One of the first things we are taught as instructors is the concept of "monitor and adjust." The best class plans can change in a moment, depending on how the students are responding in front of you. I now had to learn how to apply that knowledge to my upcoming Korea trip as well. Up until approximately two weeks before I was to leave, the testing was going to be held five days after arriving, giving the testers a chance to acclimatize themselves. Two weeks before I was to leave, the time was changed to the morning after arriving, and for me (and I'm sure for many others) that was a big adjustment. My flight was scheduled to arrive at Incheon Airport at 4:30 PM Korean time, which was 12:30 AM of the previous day back home, and testing was scheduled for 8 AM local time the following morning. It was beginning to look like I would have my work cut out for me upon arrival.

After receiving this information, one of the first adjustments I was to make was when I was checking in online for my flight. During the process of confirming my flight, I received a prompt asking if I wished to upgrade to first class, something I had never considered in the past. I thought, why not look at what the difference in price was? It turned out to be an additional $800, but I decided to take the upgrade. I figured, if I was going to be flying nonstop for twelve hours and testing the morning after arriving, it would be worth the extra cost. I wanted to give myself the best chance of succeeding. In all my years of airline travel, I had always wondered what it would be like to travel first class. I was about to find out. It was a great experience and very enjoyable; I was confident I'd arrive in much better spirits than if I'd flown economy. I enjoyed the experience so much that I upgraded to first class on my return flight too.

Upon arriving, I was picked up and driven to our host hotel in Seoul. The rooms were about half the size of a North American hotel and I shared it with one of our senior ranks for my stay. Although space was a little tight, overall it was an enjoyable experience.

The next morning arrived far too quickly, but on the bright side, the testing was being held in the same hotel. I was able to get up early, have a light breakfast, and go to the area where the testing would take place. I could then loosen up a bit and get the blood flowing through my muscles. So far, I hadn't felt much if any jet lag, so that at least was promising. Gradually, the room began to fill with other testers; I believe there were about thirty of us that morning. The judging panel that morning consisted of our Grand Master (ninth degree), a couple of Chief Masters (eighth degree), and four Senior Masters (seventh degree), who had also made the trip. At 8 AM, we were ready to get underway. For the most part, considering the flight the day before, the time change, and the different environment, I felt my testing was respectable. The only hiccup was that I didn't break one board until my third attempt, which meant I would receive only one point. If I got a four on my form and a three on my sparring, I could still make my eight.

After the testing, we spent the next ten days experiencing the Korean culture and the birthplace of taekwondo. Every day included some aspect of training as we travelled to various schools and universities around Korea. We spent a night in a Buddhist monastery eating dinner and then breakfast with the monks. The monastery, as you can imagine, had a very peaceful, serene atmosphere, which was juxtaposed with artillery fire from a military base nearby—an interesting experience. North Korea is never far from their thoughts. We did a lot of travelling by bus to see various sight and cities on the Korean peninsula. The four words I came to hate the most during our time there were "back on the bus." But all in all, I'm glad I went and I'm appreciative for the experience. While there, I considered taking a trip to the Demilitarized

Zone, which borders North Korea. From Seoul, it's only about one hour away, but I couldn't bear another bus ride. When I am inducted as a Master this June, I may look at returning to Korea and making that trip.

Returning home, it was right back to working on the business while I waited to receive my score. I knew chances were slim but I was hopeful that somehow I'd been able to pull it off and earn the required points. Even though I had my doubts, I was still disappointed a few weeks later when I found out that I had missed a passing score by one point, but it was what it was. Knowing that I had to stay on track, the only thing to do was book my flight and room for Little Rock and begin preparing myself to do another mid-term there. No, I didn't fly first class.

Even though our requirements state that we only need to pass three mid-terms, when I passed my fifth degree test, I made a commitment to myself that no matter what I would mid-term every year for the required five years in rank, even if I received my three passing scores. It was a good thing I made that commitment, because I would use up all five of my mid-terms plus one more before I got my three passing scores. I am not a person to put my training on hold or take time off because I'd met the minimum requirements. Doing the minimum or stopping because of disappointment is not the mark of success. My core values of being "relentless" and "resilient" would serve me well over the next five years, as I would draw on them repeatedly during the challenging times to come.

As soon as I received my results, I began to train for Worlds. In all my years of training, this period would be the hardest. It wasn't just the results of my mid-terms but also learning how to adjust and accept things that I had no control over. The Korea trip and the change of the testing day would set the tone for the next five years. Arriving at Worlds in 2013, I again felt prepared and ready. I felt I had trained to the best of my abilities and knowledge. I was looking forward to another chance to take that first step towards my sixth degree. Over the days leading up to the testing day, I would get down to the site and go over my material, physically working on my form on the mats, doing some shadow sparring, and visualizing breaking all my boards. I felt ready. It would be held Friday night, July 24, after the Top Ten/

World Champion competitions. We were to be at the testing site and allowed inside by 7 PM.

That year's World Championship ran overtime and the testers would not get inside until after 8 PM. For over an hour, four hundred or so black belts of all ranks, ages 17 and up, were stuck in a hallway in the Little Rock Convention Center. It was hot, crowded, and for me draining. I had prepared for everything but this. By the time we got inside and the testing started, it was 8:30. The first thing we did was the fit test. I did well, but I pushed too hard and it burned me out. My form was shaky, my sparring poor, and again, even though I broke all my boards, I didn't break them first time. I received a six. For someone who'd had only two non-passing scores in thirteen previous mid-term testing's, having two within a period of four months was disappointing beyond words.

In my sixty-six years, I had dealt with many disappointing times. The difference now was that receiving those two scores within such a short period of time motivated me even more. My training gave me the resilience that had been lacking in my life before Songahm and, as disappointing as it was, I became more committed than ever to find a way through. I knew I would find away to regroup.

An option that the American Taekwondo Association had instituted in the last year was being able to do a mid-term at a regional Elite Instructor Training Camp or a Rank Advancement Training (RAT) camp. I had attended a couple in the past year for training and to improve my overall knowledge, but I had never thought of doing a mid-term at one. The following April of 2014, I registered for one down in Oregon, thinking to change my fortune. Both camps, Elite and RAT, are composed of training for three hours on Friday night, then training all day Saturday from 9:00 AM to 6:00 PM with the testing being done in the last hour late Saturday afternoon. The camps are great for training, but they are also a test of one's physical and mental endurance. That day I was up to the challenge. I scored an eight, my first passing mark on my way to sixth, but I would still need to get a passing score where it mattered either at a national event or at Worlds.

Almost every year, I attend the World Championship to take courses, compete, or do a mid-term or test as required. The one in 2014 would be no different. After receiving my passing score, I booked my flight and room, and registered for another mid-term. Receiving a passing score from a RAT camp or Elite Instructor camp where you may test in front of one or two high rank judges from HQ is not the same as standing in front of twelve to fifteen high rank judges at Worlds or Spring or Fall Nationals. Passing at a regional camp is good for the spirit, but the national events are a more accurate accounting of one's abilities to deal with and handle pressure.

The 2014 testing was held on the morning of Thursday, July 10, and the fit test would be done after testing was over. I felt ready; I always train in the morning, so this was right in my prime time. I'd come prepared, or so I thought. I couldn't have been more wrong or disappointed. First I blew up my form. *Poomsae* (pattern), form is one of my favorite disciplines; I still today cannot figure out how I did what I did, getting all turned around, something I'd never done before or since. That day I did. My sparring was respectable and, even though I had always broken my boards, even if it was on the third attempt, this time I didn't, giving me a zero. In all my years of training, I had never missed breaking a hand technique, but I did that day. I was devastated, thoroughly disappointed with myself. I walked back to my hotel trying to find something, anything positive about my performance to hang my hat on, but it was a struggle.

The next morning I didn't even want to get out of bed. I was registered to compete in the Top Ten. I no more felt like competing than I did jumping off a bridge, but somehow I was able to motivate myself to get up and go. I'm glad I did; that morning, I won my second World Championship in weapons with my cane form. That success took some of the sting out of the previous day's performance and reminded me that every day is a new day and, when we can remember to put our best foot forward, good things can happen.

Three weeks later, I would receive my fourth mid-term score: a five, my worst score ever. I had completed four mid-terms with one passing score, and that one done at a regional camp. I was down and looking for answers, but for the moment nothing was coming. More than ever, I had to pick myself up and use every ounce of discipline and experience to work this thing through. If nothing else, I am persistent; those two core values of relentlessness and resiliency would definitely need to be applied, and I would draw on both of them over the coming months.

Later that fall, I learned of an Elite Instructor camp taking place in Surrey, BC, in February of 2015. One of the requirements of Mastership is that you have to be a sixth degree; another is that your instructor certification must also be current. In Songahm, an instructor must recertify every three years. If our certification expires and we don't recertify, we are not permitted to test or advance until we are current. Attending this camp would allow me to renew my instructor certification and also do another mid-term. As I'd had success the last year doing a mid-term at one, I looked to see if I could do it again. I had to continue to take positive steps even if they were small. That day I was able to accomplish both, scoring an eight on my mid-term and renewing my teaching certificate as well. Once again, I booked a flight, a room, seminars, and the mid-term application for Worlds and continued my training. Ever since I was a third degree, I had made a point of mid-terming or rank testing at one of the national events, and I had always scored well, but with my score from Korea and my last two trips to Worlds, it seemed I was going backwards somehow. I had to change this, and soon.

I was now in my sixty-eighth year. On Friday, July 10, at Worlds 2015, I once again found myself preparing to see if I could achieve something that up until the last two years I'd had no trouble accomplishing, that of receiving a passing score from a test or mid-term at a national event. Rank/mid-term testing's at Worlds are generally composed of four hundred or so black belts, 17 and above, ranging in rank from first to seventh degree. We are broken up by age and rank into groups of approximately forty to fifty testers, and then put in pods. In each pod, there are four rings, allowing four competitors at a time to demonstrate their material. Each pod has its own judging panel, anywhere from twelve to fifteen high rank judges (sixth degree Masters to ninth degree Grand Masters).

When doing the form portion of our testing, we are brought up in groups of four to demonstrate our forms. The presentation of forms is done from youngest to oldest, and usually there will be an odd number at the end. Instead of four, you might have two or three in the last group. That day, when the floor conductor called for the last group, my name was the only one. I would be the last tester on the floor for forms. The judges put me right in the middle of the pod. At first, I was a little unnerved to say the least. All eyes were on me—my black belt peers, their friends and family, and the complete panel of judges. If you have ever had to speak or perform on your own in front of a group, I'm sure you get the picture.

Immediately, I could feel the adrenaline starting to surge through my body. There are ninety-five moves in *Chung Hae*, the fifth degree form. I was so amped up that, when given the command to start, I almost missed a technique right away but was able to adjust and recover. A few more techniques in, while doing a three-kick combination on one leg, I began struggling with my balance. I remember reminding myself to slow down, which I was able to do. Once I found my rhythm, I completed my form without any more challenges. I don't recall anything until I heard the floor conductor say *bah-ro*, which in Korean means "end," and then the applause from my peers and the spectators. I felt good.

Upon completing my form, the Center Judge called me up to the head table. This was not normal, as usually there are four students on the floor at the same time. I didn't know what to expect, so I just said, "Yes, Sir" and ran up to the head table. When I got there, he asked where I was from and who my instructor was. When I told him I was from Canada and who my instructor was. He simply gave me a fist bump and told me "I was the man." Many of the other judges followed his lead with the fist bump and compliments. Walking back to the edge of the pod, I was elated. There are no words to describe how much those words meant to me. The rest of that testing flew by and, even though I still didn't break all my boards on my first attempt, I was confident that I would receive a passing score. A few weeks later, I received my mark—a nine, which meant if I had broken my boards in the first attempt, I would have receive a perfect score. I couldn't have written a script any better on how I would want to pass my final mid-term. The way was now clear for me to test the next year in July of 2016 for my sixth degree and look to become a Master Candidate. I was one step away from accomplishing my goal.

Even before receiving my mark, I made a point of reaching out to the Center Judge. I wanted to let him know just how much his words and actions had meant to me. The last two years of disappointment and frustration were erased, and I had a new lease on my training and commitment. His actions that day helped to reinforce my belief that, at all times, I needed to pay attention to what I did and said. To remember just how much impact my words and deeds can have on another soul, both in a negative or positive way. It was a reminder for me to make sure that, in going forward, to always do my best to ensure my words and actions always lift people up and motivate them.

In November of 2015, I submitted my application to HQ with Senior Master Ford's blessing for approval to test for my sixth degree on July 1, 2016—Canada Day. If approved, I would be testing with three fellow Canadian students I had trained with over the years under Senior Master Ford. It was going to be great. If we all passed, we would all be in the same master's class. In March of 2016, I received my approval and again booked flights, hotel, and seminars, and trained, trained, trained—I wanted a ten.

On the morning of July 1, I was once again one of a few hundred black belts from around the world. We had all come together in Little Rock for the same reason, to challenge ourselves to achieve a higher standard. The pod that I was in had three of the four Canadians testing for their sixth that day. I felt mine went okay; my form was strong, my sparring respectable, although once again I didn't break my boards the first time. I knew the best I could get would be a nine, but if I could nail the fit test I could potentially get back the point I'd lost on my boards. I pushed myself with everything I had left and finished the fit test in six minutes—a minute under my required time—if nothing else, I felt I had not lost a point. Doing the fit test right after a testing just hammers you and, by the end, I was close to being sick.

Three weeks later, Senior Master Ford phoned me to tell me that I had received a "no change." I was not surprised, but I was again disappointed. I also found out that only one of the four of us passed.

MASTERSHIP

When I was preparing to test at Worlds, I knew that no matter, whether I passed or failed, I would be travelling to Orlando in October for the Fall Nationals. If I passed, I would be going to begin my Master's training. If I didn't, I would be going to retest.

At 7:30 AM on the morning of Oct 21, 2016, I was nervous, so nervous that I arrived at the ESPN Wide World of Sports tournament site at 6:15 AM, a little over an hour early, hoping to get on the mats to get a feel for them and loosen up. But I was too early. They didn't open the gates till after 7:00 AM, so along with a few other early arrivals, I did what I could to get loose. Once allowed in, I found the pod that would be where I was to test. Once again, I would be joined by the two other instructors from Canada who had also "no changed" at Worlds. We were able to have a quick chat and wish each other good luck before we were called to line up. I had not lined up to test in front of Grand Master since the Korea trip, now there were two of them, not to mention the other high rank judges who were all Chief Masters, many of them part of the Founders Council—men and women, all eight degrees who had been there at the beginning with Eternal Grand Master and the creation of Songahm Taekwondo. I would test in front our most senior ranks; as nervous as I was, in my heart I knew, if I passed, I would have been passed by the best and, if I received another "no change," I would have received it from the best. All I could do was focus my mind and energy, and do my best. Forms are always done first and mine felt good and strong—first part complete. Next was sparring. My first partner was a young sixth degree Master (face it, from where I am, they're all young). He was a great partner. We went back and forth, timing each other out. It was a great match, and my second partner was much the same. I had completed two of the requirements and was feeling pretty good, but my nemesis was waiting for me—my boards. I had chosen my breaks two off my left side and two from my right side, one hand and one foot off each side. I felt if I was truly going to wear a sixth degree black belt I should be able to be as effective with my left, my weaker side, as I was with my right, my strong side. So I set them up in a circle much like a combat situation with multiple attackers. First was the left hook, slight turn, right cross, slight turn, left round kick, slight turn, right side kick. I broke them all first time. Boy was I happy; it was a great relief. It had been many years since I'd broken all my boards on the first attempt. For the first time in a long time, I was confident that, this time, I had passed my test.

Three weeks later I received a text from Senior Master Ford with two stars, his way of letting me know I'd passed. I was now officially a Master Candidate. It was one of the proudest moments of my life—I received my perfect ten. I had done it; I had reached the goal I'd set twenty years ago. I would soon receive my invitation to become a Master Nominee. I had once again overcome the odds and persevered through the challenges and disappointments of the last five years, just as I had done twenty years before. I had overcome bankruptcy and was able to start a new life. In February of 2017, I would attend the Spring Nationals to formally start my Master's training, and if I met all the requirements, I would be formally inducted by the Grand Master as a Master Instructor on June 21, 2017, at the World Expo in Little Rock. What a tremendously satisfying feeling! I believe in my heart of hearts that this accomplishment was made possible because I was able to remain healthy, strong, and fit in the three main areas of my life—mental, physical, and emotional.

May 2013 Korea trip demo team performing on the mall in Seoul in front of Grand Master In Ho Lee

MASTERSHIP

Standing beside the bust of Eternal Grand Master H.U. Lee in front of the Vision Wall; in the Gate and Garden in Little Rock, Arkansas, where I would be inducted as a Master

CHAPTER 13
HEALTH CHALLENGES

"Physician heal thyself."

—*Luke 4:23*

Over my years of training, I've had to deal with challenging health issues. One of the most interesting things that I came to learn from my studies is that martial artists were traditionally known as healers. To the casual observer, the arts seem to focus primarily on fighting and developing ones self-defence skills. We've all seen the movies with the flashy kicks, agility, and ability to fight off multiple adversaries at once. On closer examination, you don't have to look far to discover that many martial arts practitioners were also healers. This could entail anything from the setting of bones to massage, to the study of medicinal herbs and medicines. To quote from *The Warrior as Healer* by Thomas Richard Joiner, "Traditional martial arts training placed as much emphasis on nurturing the spirit as it did on honing fighting ability. This extended to the study of the healing arts and the uses of herbs, not only for injury management but also to increase sensitivity, improve energy levels, and most significantly, raise consciousness." In my training over the years, I have had the opportunity to personally practice and learn more about this little known part of the arts. If you are interested in learning more, simply Google "Martial artists as healers" and you will come up with all kinds of information.

In the spring of 2000, I discovered I was in need of some healing information due to a health issue. I've been sick before and like most I went to my doctor for a solution, but once I started my training, my perspective changed on how I would deal with health challenges. I learned to accept and take responsibility for what was happening with my body and mind, and have come to understand my role and responsibility in the care of both.

I will talk about two instances here, one early on in my second life and one just before I was to go to Orlando to retest for my sixth degree.

The first real health challenge occurred shortly after I had received my first degree belt. It started slowly with a small irritating rash on my forearms that, when scratched, became inflamed and spread. I had no idea what was causing this rash, but it would weep and fester whenever I scratched it. At its worst, it would cover as much as fifty percent of my body. The only places that seemed immune to it were my face and back. It was on the top and bottom of my feet, the backs of my legs, my chest and shoulders, the palms of my hands, and my forearms. It expressed itself differently in different places. Some areas were dry and scaly, and others were filled with lymph and would weep if I irritated the area by scratching. The tops of my feet would become incredibly itchy and, when I would scratch, my skin would get a little red, but a rash wouldn't show up until the next day. It was all incredibly irritating and uncomfortable.

One of the first things I did was go to my doctor. He didn't really have an answer so he referred me to a skin specialist. The two doctors I went to did not seem to have an answer either. All they did was give me some steroid creams that did little but mask the symptoms and, as soon as I stopped applying them, the rash would flare up again, usually worse. To be honest, I find that many in the medical professions are so overwhelmed with all the different health challenges being presented to them in today's world that they are left with just trying to treat the symptoms rather having the time to get to the root cause.

For me, there did not seem to be a ready answer or solution. So I began to work on determining the cause myself and hopefully finding a solution; it was my body after all. At this point, I had been training for over three years and I was slowly beginning to rebuild and recreate my life. I realized that the style of my life was gradually changing and the thought came to me that maybe my old style of living and thinking was clashing internally with my new lifestyle. Was it possible that this internal conflict was expressing itself through my skin? All the accumulated stresses and suppressions of the previous twenty or so years in music were now literally rising to the surface of my skin, and there was nothing to hold them back.

That may seem odd, but once that thought came to me, it made perfect sense on a deeper level. The two lifestyles were diametrically opposed to one another. The world of music that I had been living involved a loose bohemian lifestyle. All the while, we were striving for that big break, ready to do whatever it took to write that hit song or put ourselves in front of that one person who might be willing and able to help us. It was the non-stop touring and dead head driving twenty-four hours straight to get to the next gig. It was getting set up to play, then tearing down and moving on to the next job—week after week, month after month, and year after year.

Martial arts, on the other hand, although physically challenging and strenuous, are more focused on finding one's inner strength and abilities. With that concept in mind, I began to work through my frustration, disappointment, and anger, the health issues that were associated with those emotions such as hypertension, my attitude and poor diet, which I had ignored in my previous life.

I started by going back and reflecting on the things I'd done over my years of playing music, my nonchalant attitude to towards a great many things, thoughts, diet, sleep etc . I juxtaposed that with what I was presently doing. I began studying my diet and paying attention to what I was putting into my body and mind. I started paying attention to how my body reacted after eating certain things. If my skin would react negatively or flair up after eating something I would start eliminating it from my diet for a time to see if it would improve.

Two things I loved to drink, coffee and milk, were dropped from my diet during this time. Kona coffee was a great start every day, as it gave me a good morning boost and amped me up. I loved the smell of it and still do, and I enjoyed the flavor. With milk, I began noticing it was unsettling to my stomach, something I had never noticed before. Both of these seemed to increase the stress on my body. By simply eliminating them, I noticed that my skin became quieter for longer periods and my overall anxiety level lessened.

It didn't have an immediate effect on the rash, but over time along with the other steps I would take it allowed my skin to heal. I had stopped drinking alcohol and smoking many years earlier. Over the next year, I began to open myself up and consider improvements to my diet, which I had always been resistant to. I began to eat more raw vegetables, which before I wouldn't have done. I cut out drinking all soft drinks and began drinking only water and juice.

Over my fifty-three years, I had seldom given much thought to what I put in my body or for that matter what I'd allowed into my mind. As I continued to train and study, I began to see things in a much different light. Health is, as I came to understand it, a mental paradigm that expresses itself through our bodies, thoughts, and actions. What I was experiencing, I came to believe, was a result of what I was condoning through thoughts, actions and diet, and it became contingent on me to work through this problem and find a solution to this challenge.

It was a painstaking and at time arduous daily journey that took well over a year to clear up. Even today, if I become overstressed, my forearms will flare up. My skin has now become my early warning system, letting me know I am pushing too hard and losing my mental and emotional equilibrium.

I have been rash-free for almost fifteen years now without the assistance of the medical system. I never went back to my own doctor regarding my skin but every so often when I go to see him he will inquire as to how my skin is doing and is pleased that the problem was solved. Don't get me wrong, I am not criticizing the medical profession. I have nothing but the greatest respect for those men and women. I wouldn't have the health I have today without them, but sometimes we know our bodies better than anyone, doctors included, and we must learn to take responsibility for our health and personal well-being, from the food/fuel we put into our bodies to the thoughts we allow ourselves to think. I needed those skin specialists; they were a gift that helped motivate me to take action, which I did. Without them, who knows where I'd be. I need my doctor to bounce ideas off regarding what I'm experiencing and what I perceive to be happening in and to me. He helps guide me in the decisions I am considering and makes sure I stay on top of my annual checkups. Over the last twenty-plus years, I have come to understand that I have a personal responsibility regarding my health and it's contingent upon me to be accountable.

I have learned so much about myself and my mind through the experience of healing my skin. My overall health has improved dramatically by me becoming more conscious of my diet and sleep patterns, and staying in tune with my spirit and body. That includes not only what I put into my body, but what I do with it as well. I am also consciously aware of my thoughts and how I'm thinking. As I've heard and read many times throughout my life, "thoughts are things." What and how I think can and will lift me up or pull me down. I've learned that what I eat is the fuel that my body uses to energize itself.

> **"As I've heard and read many times throughout my life, 'thoughts are things.'"**

My second health issue came seventeen years later in the summer of 2016, after I'd returned from Worlds. This time it would involve the medical profession again but it would still be contingent on me knowing what was happening to my body and exercising the options that were available to facilitate healing.

That summer when I went back to school. I wanted to learn more about the body and how to train it more effectively, so I enrolled in a personal trainer course. It was challenging, having not been in a classroom setting for a great many years other than weekend seminars. The major challenge though was to come from the training part of the course and had to do with my body, not from my studies. This challenge would again set me on the path of personal and medical self-discovery.

Part of our training to become a certified personal trainer was learning all the different ways of accessing potential clients' challenges. On a sunny August morning, we left the classroom for a casual mile run to a local park, where we would practice some of the assessment methods like timing wind sprints, crossovers, and vertical jumps etc. After about an hour and a half of physical study and assessment practice, we ran back to the classroom for our lunch break. After lunch, we were in the classroom doing other strength and stability assessments. My body felt fine and I'd not had any problem keeping up with the other students, most of whom were in their early twenties—can't seem to get away from being the old guy! Once we had practiced and explored all the different methods of assessment, we sat back down to work out of our textbooks. After sitting for an hour, I got up to move and almost fell over. My left knee would not straighten; it was as if the whole lower leg was seized up. Very slowly, I began to flex it and was eventually able to bend and straighten the knee and move the leg. It seemed to improve and I figured that I'd just pushed it too hard. However, day after day, if I sat for extended periods, it would do the same thing. When I stood up, I had to do so very carefully and, after about three or four days of this, I got concerned. I needed to find out what was happening to my leg. I could feel something going on from my knee down to my ankle every time I was training. I didn't know if it was serious; I didn't think it was, but I wasn't sure so I went to see my doctor. In two months, I would again be travelling to test for my sixth degree. I had to get some answers, and quickly. It seemed whenever I was walking or training, it felt stable and strong, but when I would kick on the wave masters, sometimes I would feel a restriction, a tension from my knee to my ankle. That was becoming concerning for me; I needed to know what was happening. The last thing I wanted to do was pull, tear or strain a muscle with Fall Nationals so close. Also, since sitting for any length of time caused my knee to seize up, I had to constantly be careful when I was standing up. After a week of no improvement and sitting a lot in class, I phoned my doctor. When I saw him, we discussed what it could be. We agreed that we didn't think it was anything serious. Still, we thought it best that I see a sports medicine doctor, just to be on the safe side. He set up an appointment for me a week later.

As you may have noticed, other than my doctor, I am skeptical of the medical profession. My skepticism was only re-enforced with this sports medicine doctor. I know I'm in my late sixties, but I train hard, certainly not overweight, and I have a very solid core; I take what I do seriously. I expect to be treated seriously. When I saw the doctor, I concisely told her the problem I had been experiencing and explained why I was training. After examining my left knee and calf for about twenty minutes, she told me there was nothing seriously wrong, which was good, but then went on to say, "Well, this is to be expected as you get older." Honestly, a professional like you and that's all you can say? No here are some exercises that will help, nothing. Believe me when I say I was not happy (that's my polite voice speaking). She had simply written me off. I politely and respectfully left her office and never went back.

I returned to my doctor, told him about my visit, and we discussed some other options. The one thing we were both reassured about was that the doctor was in agreement with us that it didn't appear to be anything serious. We concluded that it was probably a muscle imbalance in my lower leg. I asked him about hiring a personal trainer as well as going to a massage therapist to work on the muscles of the calf. He supported everything I mentioned and gave me a prescription to see a therapist of my choosing. I also asked to have an MRI done on the knee if necessary and he agreed, giving me a prescription for that as well. Over these years, learning how to tune into my body has given me a confidence to trust what I'm doing and feeling.

Within the week, I had a personal trainer and had found a physiotherapist next door to the gym. There was improvement within a week as the knee and calf began to loosen up. I also went to see my chiropractor to have him work on my lower back. I never did get an MRI done on the knee because I didn't need it. Between the three treatments of massage, personal training three days a week for a month, and a weekly visit to the chiropractor right after having my massage treatment, there was steady improvement. Within the month, my leg had pretty much returned to what it was before the day of training back in mid-August. I could sit for a while, get up, and move as comfortably as I had before. By the time I flew down to Orlando, I had been training full-on for well over two weeks and was quite comfortable sitting on the flights. When I got up to walk, there were no issues. I was ready to go.

These past twenty years have taught me a great many things, including just how important the quality of my life and my health is, not only to me but to my family, loved ones, and friends and that it's on me to take care of it. As I continue to work towards my Mastership, I have had to overcome a great many obstacles—some physical, some mental, and some regarding my health. All of them were challenging, but I realize now that my mind and my body are mine to care for, and no one else's. What I allow into them is what I will get back in return.

My body is my personal temple. I live in it every day of my life. I know it better than any doctor ever will, and as long as I listen to it and care for it properly, I should be able live a healthy and happy life for a long time.

Me in 2000, age 52

Me in 2015, age 67

CHAPTER 14
DEVELOPING A PASSION FOR LEADERSHIP

> "If your actions inspire others to dream more, learn more, do more and become more, you are a leader."
>
> —*John Quincy Adams*

Of all the things I expected to be introduced to through training in martial arts, leadership was not one of them. This was one of the most unexpected and surprising aspects of my training, and as much as declaring bankruptcy would guide me to Songahm, training in Songahm would guide me into the study of leadership. This was an unexpected gift, and it became just as intriguing and motivational to me as the study of martial artists as healers.

Along my twenty-year journey through the arts and business, and attaining the title of Master Instructor, I not only learned how to deal with the challenges each day would bring, but I also learned to recognize the challenges brought on by the successes in each day. These two aspects of living every day have the potential to distract us from our goal, from remaining focused on the bigger picture. They can cause us to lose track of our vision, wander off the path, and end up compromising ourselves from what we most value and from what we set out to do in the first place. For me, learning how to become more disciplined in my life and in my faith through my failures and triumphs has greatly helped me stay the course. It helped guide me into my role and my appreciation of this concept called leadership.

I have come to hold my personal leadership development as a key component in my pursuit of becoming a Master. Where I started from to where I am today has been a gradual evolution. It was not something I planned or conceived of, nor was it something I set out to do, but along my journey I became an avid learner. In recognizing and accepting that I have many faults and weaknesses, for me, the only way I could hope to improve was by learning and studying. Urban Meyer encapsulated this concept best when he stated that "Leaders are learners."

> **"Leaders are learners."**
> **—Urban Meyer**

I have learned and experienced much through my mistakes and victories in my position as the leader of our company. I've learned to become more disciplined and to work through financial misjudgments while keeping my life and our business in order. I've learned to pay the price for a careless comment or action, and to take ownership of it and then be prepared to see the mistake through to a successful resolution. Learning how to watch our bank account grow yet be disciplined in the proper allocation of funds is essential to proper fiscal planning. I've learned to be disciplined, trying to set the best possible personal example every day for our students, parents, and staff—though at times failing miserably, I still have so much to learn.

When thinking about my position as a leader, I've come to realize just how many of our students have been training with us for more than half their lives. That's a tremendous commitment of trust from our parents, a strong sense of dedication from our students, and a challenging responsibility to live up to as a staff. Being able to accept, understand, and acknowledge this responsibility and the influence we have in helping shape their lives is at times very humbling and inspiring; many's the time it has given me pause to reflect and be extremely grateful. As I grew to accept a greater understanding of my position of responsibility, I realized that it was important for me to do my

MASTERSHIP

utmost to exemplify the valued leadership skills of Songahm such as courtesy, respect, loyalty, and self-discipline. Just as important, though, was to learn how to give our students the opportunity to develop their own leadership skills.

I began to focus on how we could educate our students responsibly and guide them to discover their own sense of leadership so they could successfully lead themselves. I thought it important to introduce them to people like Malala Yousafzai, Rosa Parks, Mahatma Gandhi, Nelson Mandela, and Martin Luther King, Jr., to name a few, in the hope of inspiring them to search for and identify leaders who they may wish to emulate one day or future leaders who they may choose to follow and support.

In this position of responsibility, I wrestle with the question: how do we equip our students to deal with the world of tomorrow? This has become an ongoing challenge for me. In public school, children learn the necessary skills to help them in the world at large, but there is little about leadership skills development. I wanted to find a way to give them some leadership skills and practical experience as I believe this is a key to their future success and our country's.

The leadership program our governing body created revolves around what we term the three Ps: public speaking, presentation, and performance. The more I personally studied leadership, the more I wanted a program that covered these three aspects and more. I believe that strong, effective leadership is one of the underlying fundamentals of the freedoms we enjoy in our country, even though at times we may strongly disagree with some of those who lead us. It seems in many ways that leadership has become more about winning at all costs than truly learning to lead, the personality ethic versus the character ethic. Obviously, if we are a leader, our goal is to motivate our team to win. I know when I compete, I want to win or, when any of our students compete, I want them to compete to win, but winning at any cost, regardless of morals or ethics is for me simply unacceptable. My thought in this regard is "to compete is to learn."

> **"To compete is to learn."**
> **—Lorne Davidson**

MASTER LORNE DAVIDSON

Today, so much time and energy is spent on simply living day to day to make ends meet that it seems the only things we have the time to learn about are things that have an immediate impact on our bottom line. That's where the learning stops. But if I win and don't learn anything, where is the victory? How long does it last, if I lose but learn that knowledge has the potential to benefit me for the rest of my life?

I have achieved World Champion status three times, but as I stated earlier, two days later I competed and came in second in forms and fourth in weapons; that experience taught me that victory is short-lived. The next day, I have to be prepared to start again if my goal is duplicate it, and as a leader, that is my goal. Subtle understandings such as this are what motivated me to improve my study of leadership. I encourage our students to work to improve one percent every day; if they can learn to establish the habit of improvement, then every year they have the possibility of improving three hundred and sixty-five percent—and that's just in one year! Compound that over ten, twenty, or a lifetime; it's hard to imagine the potential of what could be accomplished.

When thinking along that line and about what could be accomplished with gradual, incremental improvement I came across the Top Five Regrets of people who were at the end of their life. I've included these as a reminder of the benefits that come from taking time in our lives to be reflective, which I make sure to do while continuing to contribute in my position as a leader. I believe it important to never forget that no one gets off this rock alive; when my day comes, I want to make sure I have led my life not only to the best of my talent and abilities but also from my heart. The comments at the end are mine.

1. I wish I'd had the courage to live a life true to myself, not the life others expected of me; another way I've heard it expressed is "I wished I'd taken more risks"—I've always followed my heart, even to my detriment.

2. I wished I hadn't worked so hard—a work in progress to work smarter

3. I wished I'd had the courage to express my feelings—in some areas good, in others working on it

4. I wished I had stayed in touch with my friends—my true friends I'm good with

5. I wished that I had let myself be happier—working on it; I've been told I'm too serious

My initial education into leadership began early by reading books when I was in my teens written by men who I admired, like John F. Kennedy (*Profiles in Courage*) and some of the great philosophers like Plato and Socrates. During my years in music, that education took a hiatus, but then I was reintroduced to it when I began my taekwondo training. Since picking up my study again, I've read books by sport coaches like John Wooden, Urban Meyer, and Pete Carroll; inspirational speakers like John Maxwell and Martin Luther King, Jr.; and authors such as Simon Sinek and Jim Collins. As well, I have read books by people whom I had heard about but wasn't too sure of, like Robert Gates and Donald Rumsfeld. I read the autobiographies of Mahatma Gandhi, John D. Rockefeller, and Nelson Mandela. I watched inspiring biographical movies like *Freedom Writers*, *We Were Soldiers*, *Cry Freedom*, and *Remember the Titans*. Some were about great men and women, but many were about regular people like you and me.

As a leader and a learner, I am always asking questions. I'll ask questions about how to improve personally as a father, a husband, an instructor, or a businessman. As a leader, I can't ever be satisfied or defeated by my successes or failures. As our Grand Master Emeritus

---

TOP FIVE REGRETS

1. I wish I'd had the courage to live a life true to myself, not the life others expected of me; another way I've heard it expressed is "I wished I'd taken more risks"

2. I wished I hadn't worked so hard

3. I wished I'd had the courage to express my feelings

4. I wished I had stayed in touch with my friends

5. I wished that I had let myself be happier

quoted, "There's always more to learn." Learning has become a strong focus in my life, probably stronger than at any other time.

Being in this position, I believe that learning, and the desire to learn, is the most valuable thing that I can share with our students—to do that, I must model it by leading proactively. Over my years of training and discovery, I have often had times where I questioned my words and actions, and I came to realize that, if I wanted any situation to improve, I had to start with me; my words had to be backed up by my actions.

I came to understand that leadership was about being proactive when dealing with challenges or problems. It was learning how to handle success and not let it go to my head, not letting myself think or believe that I had it all figured out. Learning how to balance the two ends of the same stick (failure and success) helped me develop my personal leadership skills. My training in Songahm Taekwondo, I realized, taught me a great deal about balance, not just developing strong stances or balancing on one leg while executing a kick or two, but maintaining a balance between the left and right sides of my body and what takes place between my ears.

That was one of the motivating factors in my choice of board breaks for my sixth degree. Being able to execute one hand and one foot technique successfully from each side of my body was important for me as it would demonstrate a balance, the ability to be effective from either side of my body with both my hands and feet.

Leadership, for me, is also about developing our ability to be observant, to be able to adjust to a given situation while still holding to our original course of action, the ability to monitor and adjust, to think on our feet and still succeed by getting the job done.

As my experience and skill developed, I began to share this knowledge with our students. I encouraged them to start exercising their own observation skills and watch how they dealt with success and failure, as well as what's going on around them. Not only for the purpose of self-defence, but in general, observing what's taking place around them every day, at home, at school, or with their friends. I wanted them to develop a greater awareness of what they're looking at and hearing about.

MASTERSHIP

For me, this starts with a desire to learn, as "leaders are learners"; more than anything though, if I can be successful at inspiring our students both old and young alike to want to learn, I will consider myself successful. In closing out this chapter, I want to shine a light on a couple of our students who were in our leadership program and taught me a great deal about life, its possibilities, leadership, and courage, simply by the examples they set.

The first student was a fifteen-year-old young man who had been training with us since August of 2012 and was a couple of testing's away from testing for his first degree black belt. In June of 2015, Will was diagnosed with leukemia. This was devastating news for him and his family, and everyone who trained with him, staff and students alike. We all knew Will was a fighter, but just how much of a fighter he was, we were about to find out. For many months, he was in and out of the hospital, going through chemotherapy treatments, fighting for his life. Over his time in hospital whenever I visited him, he would always have a smile and a winner's attitude, even when I knew he was scared and tired. We talked about him returning to school and completing his education and where he would go on vacation when he was well again. We talked about setting a goal for finishing his journey to black belt. He would fight the disease for many months and he eventually won that battle. Today, he is a healthy young man who successfully tested for his black belt in October of 2016 and is in the process of completing his grade 12. Throughout his battle with cancer, he became an inspiration to me and to all our students and staff. The day he returned to class, there were a few tears shed, myself included; it was great to see him well again.

The second student was a young eight year old girl who, one day when she was six, was complaining to her mom about something, to which her mom politely responded by recommending she go to her room and write down something she was grateful for. This simple recommendation apparently struck a major chord with her and she took it to heart. For the next year and a half, without telling anyone, she did this daily. One day in her eighth year, she came back to her mom and said, "Here are all the things I am grateful for." She had written out one thing every day and now had over four hundred things that she was grateful for. Today Muskan, at the ripe old age of nine, is a published author and has been travelling, when she's not in school, doing book signings and promotions with her book *365 Days of Gratitude: My Attitude of Gratitude*; it is available on Amazon. I am fortunate to have an autographed copy and have enjoyed reading it.

These two young people are examples of the quality of students whom I have had the honor and privilege to teach over these last twenty years, they are both dedicated learners.

In spending the greater part of twenty years studying leadership, I have come to the understanding that leaders of value are people who remain committed to learning. This is the main reason I continue to study and teach leadership. My goal is to inspire. For they are the leaders of tomorrow; they are tomorrow's Masters.

Some of tomorrow's Masters

MASTERSHIP

Our leadership staff

CHAPTER 15
MASTERSHIP

"You are always a student, never a master.
You have to keep moving forward."

—*Conrad Hall*

Over the last two decades, I had not given a lot of thought to what it would mean to become a Master Instructor. But since passing my sixth degree test, it seems I don't think of anything else—everything I think, say, and do is filtered through this coming accomplishment. At times, it seems surreal and overwhelming, and at other times, I can't wait for June to get here. I'd like to take a minute and say how honored I am that you, the reader, have shared and been a part of my journey simply by reading this book. Thank you.

It's Sunday, February 12, 2017. I'm sitting in the Paris Hotel in Las Vegas, waiting to be picked up by the shuttle that will take me to the airport for my flight home. At this moment, I have some time to reflect on the past twenty years. The past few days were exciting as I began taking the final steps in my training to attain the title of Master. The physical training was hard, as one would expect, but satisfying. Part of our work, though, was creating an identity for our Masters class. It is a tradition that every Masters class chooses a name for their class. At dinner a couple of nights ago, we chose to name our class the "Jinhwa Masters" (*Jinhwa* in Korean means "evolution"). This is a name I can completely identify with. On a personal level, I can relate it to my journey from being bankrupt at forty-eight to my new life at sixty-nine. From a taekwondo perspective, it would be my way of confirming my personal commitment to assisting our organization in any capacity possible in its evolution as it continues to grow and evolve. *Jinhwa* encapsulates much of what has taken place in my life over the past twenty years. It has been and I'm sure will continue to be an evolution; may it ever remain so.

I will turn seventy this August and I can honestly say that the past twenty years have been the most challenging, satisfying, and rewarding years of my life to date. In looking back to that February day in 1996 when we declared bankruptcy, I can see it was the best decision I ever made, as hard as it was at the time.

That decision brought me face to face with my actions, literally stopping in my tracks. It was from that point on that I began to re-evaluate my life, something which I continue to do to this day, reflect and re-evaluate then move forward. I had to take a hard look at my attitude of "rights versus privilege," and how my arrogance and ignorance had threatened the existence of everything I loved—my family. Second, it taught me the value of money. More importantly though, I found there is something far more valuable to me than money: self-discipline. If I have that, I can achieve whatever I set my mind to.

Quality of life does not come from how many possessions we acquire, but from how we discipline ourselves as we move through our lives. What do we take as our reason for being? What are our core values? What do we value more than anything? What gets us up in the morning? If I say money, I'm on the wrong path. For me money is simply a by-product of a fulfilled life.

Third, it taught me to recognize that we are the fortunate few. There are not many cultures or countries in the world that give us the opportunities we have to achieve our dreams or to correct our mistakes, allowing us the opportunity of a second or third chance at life. But that is only if we are willing to take the chance and go for it. We have the ability to pick up our neighbors when they have fallen because someone took the time to help us up when we fell. I would not be the man I am today if I hadn't gone bankrupt, but there were many, many people who helped me and my family along the way back to health and prosperity.

The first fifty years of my life were filled with an arrogance of knowledge. I thought I knew it all, but those years were rife with misconceptions and mistakes. I read somewhere that "if you think you know it all, you're setting yourself up for a major fall." I can attest to that as that's exactly what happened to me. Having said that, those first fifty years with all their mistakes were a gift that helped set me up for the last twenty. There is a quote that I've always enjoyed by Bill Keane: "Yesterday's the past, tomorrow's the future, but today is a gift. That's why it's called the present." What we do, what we say, and what we think contribute to what makes today "today." Every day, I work to make it count in every way I can, even if it does not turn out to be the day I'd hoped for.

> **"Yesterday's the past, tomorrow's the future, but today is a gift. That's why it's called the present."**
> **—Bill Keane**

Right now, I wanted to be hiking Red Rock Mountain with my Masters class. It's a tradition for every group at the end of the Vegas training to make that hike, but I'm sitting here writing this book. Why? Because while here in Vegas, I came down with a bug that has put me flat on my back for the past day and a half with chills and a fever. The fortunate part was that I got sick after the completion of our training; the unfortunate part was I missed being a part of the class hike up the mountain. It was initiated by Eternal Grand Master H.U. Lee as part of a student's ascent to becoming a Master in Songahm Taekwondo. It was something I'd thought about and looked forward to over the last few years since I realized how close I was to attaining Mastership.

To say I was disappointed would miss the point, but it is what it is. It was hard to get up this morning, not only because I was feeling weak and sick, but also because I wasn't with them. I had a choice though: I could feel the pain of regret or do something proactive and positive in the present. I chose to do something positive. Even though Las Vegas is a noisy, smoke-filled city, I was able to find a quiet place in the hotel to write for a couple of hours. If I've learned nothing else over these years, it's that there is always something I can do to improve my situation. Sometimes it's not the easy choice, but there's always a choice. We never know when life will rise up and smack us in the face. My only responsibility is in how I pick myself up and get back in the game.

These are the nine steps in the Mastership ceremony, and these are the nine life skills we are asked to focus on over the year in our Mastership training: Vision, Respect, Loyalty, Knowledge, Gratitude, Honor, Humility, Nobility, and Mastership. I would like to share with you the significance of each step in the ceremony and my thoughts on what they mean to me.

Vision—The gong is struck slowly nine times. Traditionally the nine strikes represent the nine color belt forms. Also the gong is a complete circle representing the beginning and the end.

Helen Keller said, "The only thing worse than being blind is having sight but no vision." This is a quote I relate to because for many years I was legally blind. With two corneal grafts in the mid-nineties, I was given my sight back. For over twenty years, my vision was bad enough that I was eligible to go to the Canadian National Institute for the Blind for training. I never went, though, because I had a dream that one day I'd see and today, thanks to medical technology, with corrective lenses I have 20/20 vision. It took over twenty years for that dream to materialize, but it did.

Vision, for me, is the ability to see what isn't there and yet believe in its possibility. I had a vision of Mastership back in 1997 and I had a vision in 2000 that one day I would own a martial arts school. Both became realities. I have had visions over that time that did not come to fruition, but I will always work on visualizing my future and doing my best with what I receive.

Respect—This is shown by the Master inductee performing three traditional Korean bows (knees and hands on the ground, forehead touching the ground between the hands) to the Grand Master. The three bows represent the inductee's mind, body, and spirit.

MASTERSHIP

This is the quality of a leader. I remember a line from the movie *Remember the Titans* when the coach tells his players, "You may not like each other, but you will learn to respect each other." We are all human beings, as John F. Kennedy said, "who breathe the same air and who share the same planet." If we are going to continue to grow as a country and as a world, even though at times we may not like each other, we must still learn to respect each other and appreciate our differences. We must develop leaders who cannot only exemplify this trait, but who can lead us and help us to learn how to do it better.

Loyalty—The inductees light their candle from the Grand Master candle, pledging their commitment to continue teaching and inspiring their students in the benefits of Songahm Taekwondo. The lit candle will constantly sacrifice itself as the body of wax melts away while keeping the flame burning. It will do so until the body no longer remains.

Jimmy Chin said, "A lot of why I climb is for the friendship, the loyalty, and trust, the shared experience of being in that moment." I have come to understand over the years that loyalty does not mean blind obedience. Along my journey, I have had the freedom to express my thoughts, joys, and concerns not only to my instructor but with the highest ranks of our organization. I've been able to do that with acceptance and without repercussion, which has instilled within me an undying loyalty to Songahm Taekwondo.

Knowledge—This following step in the ceremony is represented with water. Each inductee has three bowls in front of them, two of which are filled with water. The first is a small bowl representing that of being a student. The inductee takes this bowl and pours it into the medium-sized bowl, which represents the inductee as an instructor. The inductee then takes the medium bowl and pours the water into the largest bowl, the Master's bowl. The inductee then takes the Master's bowl and kneels in front of Grand Master to have his bowl filled with the knowledge from the Grand Master's ongoing instruction.

Confucius said, "Real knowledge is to know the extent of one's ignorance." Knowledge is a wonderful tool when coupled with experience but dangerous when isolated. Over my life, I have gained knowledge in many things, but I've had to apply it to know if it worked and then decide if it was right for me. From that I gained experience. My mother would always tell me, "Everything sounds great in theory, but you won't find out if it works until you put it into practice." In my life, I've learned a great many things the hard way simply because I thought I knew something without having the experience to go with it. When I tried, I quickly learned that I didn't know what I thought I knew. So I had to learn the hard way, from experience.

Gratitude—After the ceremonial passing of knowledge, the inductees offer a gift representing their appreciation for the knowledge, leadership, and guidance that the Grand Master has sacrificed for them in their quest for Mastership. Traditionally, the gift is a 24-karat gold coin representing loyalty and devotion. This gift is a symbol to show the worth of the student–instructor relationship.

Cicero said, "Gratitude is not only the greatest of virtues; it is the parent of all the others." There is so much in my life that I am grateful for. I'll begin with my health. I will be seventy this year; I am in the best shape of my life and enjoy my daily training. I have the energy and ability to be up between five and six every morning and put in a full day. I am grateful for my family; my wife of thirty-seven years, Carole; our three wonderful healthy children, Kat, Robyn, and Robert; and our granddaughters, Aria and Audrina. I am thankful for our home, the students and parents who put their faith and trust in us every day, the success of our business, the community, and the country we live in, and I will be forever grateful to Eternal Grand Master H.U. Lee and the Founders Council for Songahm Taekwondo. The list could go on and on; there is not a day I don't wake up grateful and feeling honored for what I have.

Honor—This step demonstrates the inductee's devotion to what is right and just, and having chosen an honorable path. In recognition

MASTERSHIP

of this, the Grand Master will place a gold Masters ring on each inductee's finger. The ring is made of 10-karat gold and black onyx inset with a diamond. The diamond represents Grand Master's loyalty to the Masters forever. Each inductee will also receive a certificate of Mastership.

Calvin Coolidge said, "No person was ever honored for what he received. Honor has been the reward for what he gave." I have heard it said that honor is something that is given, that we earn it with time. Over the past twenty years, I have had the honor to know and experience three Grand Masters and be a part of an organization that, for all its challenges, has transitioned itself successfully with each new Grand Master. When I am honored this June, I will accept the title of Master Instructor with humility and gratitude.

Humility—This is shown by the inductee's reciting of the Masters Oath; the inductee commits to dedicating themselves to their students and to Grand Master and Songahm Taekwondo.

Henri Frederic Amiel said, "There is no respect for others without humility in one's self." When Grand Master In Ho Lee dubs me a Master Instructor, I will be, as has been said, standing on the shoulders of giants. I will be forever grateful and humbled. If Eternal Grand Master H.U. Lee and the Founders Council had not created Songahm Taekwondo, I would not be who or where I am today. Along this journey, I have made friends with many exemplary people who have helped me as a martial artist, a businessman, and a human being. No one accomplishes anything on their own, and that is the truth.

Nobility—In one of the last demonstrations of the ceremony, the Grand Master dubs each inductee with the *BeeRyong Bong* (the staff of the flying dragon) finalizing the crossover from instructor to Master instructor.

Jane Porter said, "Nobility without virtue is a fine setting without a gem." Nobility is a word that speaks to character and I hope over my years of training and development that there has been an improvement in my character. Throughout my life, I have met many fine people, but my mother had the noblest of character, and I thought of her at this moment.

Mastership—In the final act of the ceremony, after being dubbed by the Grand Master, the inductees are then formally introduced to family and friends as a Master Instructor.

Richard Bach said, "What the caterpillar calls the end of the world, the master calls a butterfly." Mastership, for me, is an honored position of devotion, commitment, and service to the discipline of Songahm Taekwondo and its tenets/beliefs/principles. It is a goal achieved, but as the quotation at the beginning of this chapter reminds me, "You are always a student, never a Master. You must always keep moving forward." A Master should not only be a worthy leader proficient in their discipline, but just as important, they should be a Master of themselves. A Master is someone who has devoted decades of their life to serving and learning from those around them and those who have gone before. A true Master will never stop learning.

At the beginning of this book, I asked if you believed in second chances and if you believed you were worth a second chance. As you now know, I have many flaws and faults in my nature and I am far from perfect. I have lived with more misconceptions than I can count. If you take nothing more from this book, please realize that there are opportunities available. If it happened for me, it can happen for you. They are there, every day—we just have to want them. When they come, take hold of them and go for it with all you've got; never let them go.

When I declared bankruptcy, I had no idea what was going to happen. I was too caught up in my own frustration, anger, and disappointment to see any possibilities of what might be in front of me. It took the help and encouragement of my wife and my friend Bruce to put me in a situation where my second chance could begin to develop. Even then, it took many months before I was prepared to listen. We all have true friends around us who have our best interests at heart. We

MASTERSHIP

also have our own internal voice that wants more than anything to see us successful, if we could just learn to be quiet long enough to hear it.

I'll leave you with a quotation I found along this twenty-year journey. I repeat it to myself as a reminder regularly and have relayed it to our students ever since I started teaching. I have yet to find out who wrote it: "There is a choice we make in everything we do, but be aware that, in the end, the choice you make makes you."

Every day, we make a choice to set the mood and tone of our day. Every day, we have the choice to make our lives one percent better than the day before. It can be a day of productivity, of growth, or of frustration. My sincerest hope is that you'll make the choice to learn and grow, not just from the mistakes, but also from the successes. What will you choose to be a master of, and where will that journey take you?

> **"There is a choice we make in everything we do, but be aware that, in the end, the choice you make makes you."**
> **—Anonymous**

The three Knowledge bowls with my candle

MASTERSHIP

*Being dubbed by Grand Master In Ho Lee
inside the Gate and Garden, Little Rock, Arkansas, June 21, 2017*

My Sixth Degree Master Instructor Certificate

Being presented to family and Friends in front of the Gate after being inducted as a Master Instructor

My Mastership Ring

ACKNOWLEDGEMENTS

I would like to take a minute and give credit where credit is due; I did not accomplish this feat on my own. These are some of the most inspiring and influential people in my life who have supported and stood by me as I developed and created my second life.

    I'd like to start with my family; my wife Carole without who this journey never would have started and who remains a source of encouragement, love and support to this day, my son Robert who has not only become my partner in our company but has developed into a fine man, my daughters Kat and Robyn who became for me examples of perseverance and dedication in their lives and careers, and to our son-in-law Corey and daughter-in-law Rebecca and to our Granddaughters Aria and Audrina, my love to all of you.

    To the members of my ATA family who I have come to know over my journey and have been a continual source of guidance and inspiration throughout:

- Eternal Grand Master H.U. Lee, the man who created the opportunity for us all.
- Grand Master Emeritus Soon Ho Lee,
- Grand Master In Ho Lee,
- Grand Master G.K. Lee
- Chief Master M.K.Lee,
- Chief Master Michael Caruso,
- Chief Master Ki Seung Cho
- Sr Master Ken Church
- Sr Master Scott Karpiuk,
- Sr Master Kevin Ford,
- Master Hallie Faser,
- Master Rob Goins,
- Master Scott Turner,
- Master Russ Duer,
- Mr. Bruce McCann

    To my friends and mentors Mr. Jason Hanger, Mr. Chris Manolopoulos and Mr. Patrick Meyer who were always there with a helping hand and words of encouragement through the rough and tumble times and my good friend, Mr. Mark Donnelly.

Our parents and students, without their dedication and trust none of what you have just read would have been possible or could have taken place. Each and every one of you, both past and present hold a special place in my heart

Last but not least to the staff of the Seung-ri Academies, Mr Ben Raphael, Mr. Matthew Skaar and Ms Joni Coombs who kept our doors open and classes running smoothly under the guidance of my son Mr. Robert Davidson while I pursued this dream of Mastership, my heartfelt thanks and appreciation to each and every one of you for your inspiration, encouragement, belief and support over the years.

PERSONAL LIBRARY

BUSINESS/LEADERSHIP

An Astronaut's Guide to Life on Earth – Chris Hadfield
Mastering the Rockefeller Habits – Verne Harnish
The Obstacle Is the Way – Ryan Holiday
The West Point Way of Leadership – Col. Larry R. Donnithorne (Ret.)
21 Leadership Lessons – Richard Peddie
You Don't Have to be a Shark – Robert Herjavec
The Starbucks Experience – Joseph Michelli
The 4-Hour Work Week – Tim Ferriss
Tools of Titans – Tim Ferriss
Be Great – Peter H. Thomas
A Passion for Leadership – Robert M. Gates
Think and Grow Rich – Napoleon Hill
No B.S. Wealth Attraction – Dan Kennedy
No B.S. Business Success – Dan Kennedy
No B.S. Sales Success – Dan Kennedy
No B.S. Time Management for Entrepreneurs – Dan Kennedy
The Ultimate Sales Letter – Dan Kennedy
The Leader Who Had No Title – Robin Sharma
Secrets of the Millionaire Mind – T. Harv Eker

MASTER LORNE DAVIDSON

Like a Virgin – Richard Branson

Small Giants – Bo Burlingham

The Discipline of Market Leaders – Michael Treacy and Fred Wiersema

The Trusted Advisor – David Maister

Self-Made in America – John McCormack and David R. Legge

Jump and the Net Will Appear – Robin Crow

The Complete 101 Collection – John Maxwell

The 15 Invaluable Laws of Growth – John Maxwell

The Winning Attitude – John Maxwell

Developing the Leaders Around You – John Maxwell

Becoming a Person of Influence – John Maxwell

Developing the Leader Within You – John Maxwell

The 5 Levels of Leadership – John Maxwell

Sometimes You Win, Sometimes You Learn – John Maxwell

Failing Forward – John Maxwell

JumpStart Your Leadership – John Maxwell

Leadership 2.0 – Travis Bradberry and Jean Greaves

Turning Pro – Steven Pressfield

No Excuses! – Brian Tracy

Success is Waiting: The Martial Arts School Owner's Guide to Teaching, Business, and Life – Buzz Durkin

The No Asshole Rule – Robert I. Sutton, PhD

The Power of Tact – Peter Legge

Where Have All the Leaders Gone? – Lee Iacocca

Work the System – Sam Carpenter

MASTERSHIP

The Power of Why – Amanda Lang

Rumsfeld's Rules – Donald Rumsfeld

Rich Dad, Poor Dad – Robert Kiyosaki

The Business School – Robert Kiyosaki

Rich Dad's Cashflow Quadrant – Robert Kiyosaki

Decisions – Jim Treliving

The Secret Language of Leadership – Stephen Denning

Tell to Win – Peter Guber

Mentored by a Millionaire – Steven K. Scott

Driven from Within – Michael Jordan and Mark Vancil

Coach Wooden's Pyramid of Success – John Wooden and Jay Carty

Wooden on Leadership – John Wooden and Steve Jamison

The Essential Wooden – John Wooden and Steve Jamison

A Game Plan for Life – John Wooden and Don Yaeger

Start with Why – Simon Sinek

Leaders Eat Last – Simon Sinek

Built to Last – Jim Collins and Jerry I. Porras

Good to Great – Jim Collins

Great by Choice – Jim Collins and Morton T. Hansen

The Tipping Point – Malcolm Gladwell

Blink – Malcolm Gladwell

David and Goliath – Malcolm Gladwell

Outliers – Malcolm Gladwell

Leadership – General Rick Hillier

The E-Myth Revisited – Michael Gerber

MASTER LORNE DAVIDSON

True North – Bill George and Peter Sims

Going the Distance – Rick Hansen and Dr. Joan Laub

The 7 Habits of Highly Effective People – Stephen R. Covey

The Art of Learning – Joshua Waitzkin

Above the Line – Urban Meyer

Extreme Ownership – Jocko Willink and Leif Babin

Win Forever – Pete Carroll and Yogi Roth

AUTOBIOGRAPHY/BIOGRAPHY

Churchill – Norman Rose

Bearing the Cross (Martin Luther King, Jr.) – David Garrow

Mahatma Gandhi (Biography) – Bal Ram Nanda

Autobiography – Monhandas K. (Mahatma) Gandhi

Titan (John D. Rockefeller, Sr.) – Ron Chernow

In Search of Identity – Anwar Sadat

Long Walk to Freedom – Nelson Mandela

Robert Kennedy and His Times – Arthur M. Schlesinger, Jr.

MOVIES – AUTOBIOGRAPHY/BIOGRAPHY

Thirteen Days

Freedom Writers

Patton

Courage Under Fire

Amazing Grace

Soul Surfer

MASTERSHIP

Invincible

Coach Carter

Cinderella Man

The Hurricane

Glory Road

Invictus

Ali

Mrs Henderson

Finding Neverland

Stand and Deliver

Brother Son, Sister Moon

Cry Freedom

We Where Soldiers

ADDITIONAL INFORMATION

Bulk Sale Grouping – 10 – 49, 50 – 99, 100 – 199, 200 – 499, 500 – 1000

Available to speak to your group or organization

Contact Information:

Website – www.mastershipjourney.com
E-mail – mastershipjourney@gmail.com
Linkedin - Master Lorne Davidson
Facebook.com – mastershipjourney
Phone number – 604-542-3079

Printed in Canada